In Search of Family History

A Starting Place

Paul Drake, J.D.

Heritage Books, Inc.

Second Edition

Published 1992 By

Heritage Books, Inc.
1540-E Pointer Ridge Place
Bowie, Maryland 20716
(301) 390-7709

ISBN 1-55613-718-4

A Complete Catalog Listing Hundreds Of Titles On
Genealogy, History, And Americana
Available Free On Request

Table of Contents

Chapter 4 *Courthouses* 61

List Of Illustrations

Acknowledgments

This effort is dedicated to those students who, through requiring me to truly consider whereof I spoke, brought a level of understanding of the subject which otherwise I would not have enjoyed; to Martha for her effort with the first edition of this book; to Paul, Diane and Cheryl, who brought to me the inspiration to continue in this and all other research efforts; to dearest Brittany, Bethany, Evan, the others who will join them as grandchildren, and their yet unnamed descendants; to little Noodles, who quietly kept me company at the computer; and perhaps most of all, to Marty, who spent the many hours alone while I 'did genealogy'.

To all of you, thank you so, so much. I love you.

Paul Drake
Crab Orchard, Tennessee
August 1992

Introduction

This handbook will not teach you how to do good family research. Only practice will do that.

You will find it desirable to do interviews of relatives, to go to communities where ancestors once lived, to visit cemeteries where they rest, and to organize what you have learned from those sources and from family tales and traditions. Then, you will want to visit libraries and courthouses and add all that you can. You may want to take a course, join a society, do some writing, contribute materials and time to others and to publications, submit queries and research findings, and to ask questions of all who will answer. All the while you will be meeting some of the nicest people in the world.

When you have finished your first interview or first visit to the local library and courthouse, you will either be "hooked" on genealogy or will have decided that it is a waste of time. Incidentally, if you do not have some time to spend you have picked the wrong hobby.

Of this be sure, you and those who come after you will be proud of your ancestors and of their triumphs and failures, and will be equally proud of your work in uncovering evidence of their lives. As a result of your research, instead of remaining as mere names and dates in the family Bible, those long dead will become living, breathing human beings.

Every one of your ancestors has stories to tell, and you will come to fully understand that the emotions and feelings experienced by you were well known to those who went before. They will surprise you and eloquently speak out to you at every turn. Perhaps most of all and to your great benefit, through knowledge of those who went before, you will come face to face with your own mortality.

In a beautiful old country cemetery in Ohio there is the grave of a Welsh lady who died many years before our Civil War. Her tombstone reads:

> *Remember friend, as you pass by,*
> *What you are now, so once was I.*
> *What I am now, you will be,*
> *So prepare yourself to follow me.*

Good luck in your search!

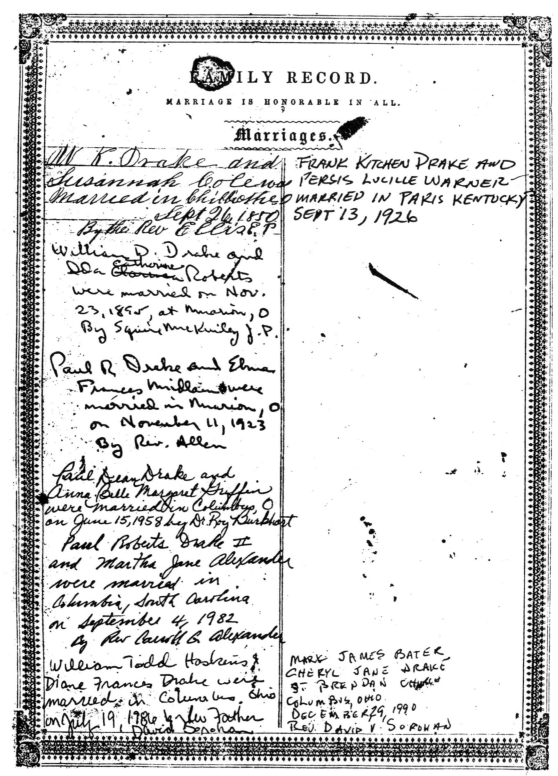

FAMILY RECORD.

MARRIAGE IS HONORABLE IN ALL.

Marriages.

W. R. Drake and Susannah Coleman Married in Chillicothe Sept 26, 1850 By the Rev. E Ellison P.

William D. Drake and Ida Catherine Roberts were married on Nov. 23, 1895, at Marion, O By Squire McKinley J.P.

Paul R. Drake and Elma Frances Midland were married in Marion, O on November 11, 1923 By Rev. Allen

Paul Dean Drake and Anna Belle Margaret Griffin were married in Columbus, O on June 15, 1958 by Dr. Roy Burkhart

Paul Roberts Drake II and Martha Jane Alexander were married in Columbia, South Carolina on September 4, 1982 By Rev Carroll G. Alexander

William Todd Hoskins & Diane Frances Drake were married in Columbus, Ohio on July 19, 1986 by her Father David Deachan

FRANK KITCHEN DRAKE AND PERSIS LUCILLE WARNER MARRIED IN PARIS KENTUCKY SEPT 13, 1926

MARK JAMES BATER, CHERYL JANE DRAKE ST. BRENDAN CHURCH COLUMBUS, OHIO. DECEMBER 29, 1990 REV. DAVID V. SOROHAN

1850 Family Bible, Marriages

Many family Bibles have been kept for long periods and, by reason of the information recorded there, should be diligently sought out by researchers. This is a page from a Bible kept from 1850 until now.

1

Thoughts on Starting

Almost all persons who have lived within the last four hundred years have left some evidence of their lives, and the search for such records can provide a delightful and inexpensive hobby. There are many sources of information, many places to go looking, and, for the most part, the search is easy. Further, since the records of past events change but very little with the passage of time, when other obligations demand it the study of family history may be put aside for long periods and then recommenced with ease.

The famous and great names of history - George Washington, Queen Elizabeth I, Ben Franklin, General Lee, and the others - left their marks in many places. For the most part, however, your ancestors were common men and women and for that reason will be somewhat more difficult to locate. Still though, the lives of common folks are every bit as interesting as are those of the wealthy and prominent, and, after all, in physical makeup and even in the way you think, speak, act, and eat, you are the genetic, cultural, and social product of each and every one of those ancestors, rich or poor, gentle or low born as they may have been.

Surely too, and most importantly, those who went before deserve better than to be reduced to the mere impersonal dates of their births, marriages, and deaths. It follows that while the gathering of dates is important and perhaps interesting, that effort is but a small part of the total task. Once gathered, we must arrange and interpret the materials uncovered in the context of the happenings - the history - of that earlier time and place, and so bring to life those who went before. By so doing you will come to realize that most of those joys, sorrows, pains, and pleasures that you feel were known equally by your ancestors.

Starting The Search

So, how do you commence? Where do you start? First off, inquire at the local library or museum concerning genealogy courses being offered in your area. Many night courses in family research are available for modest sums, and you should make every effort to enroll in one of them. They are most helpful and will provide you with guidance, assistance, and with new friends who share your interests. Even if you have been doing research for years, advanced courses will be most useful to you.

That done, the next step is to plan to keep complete records. Note taking is an absolute necessity in research, since once you have begun to uncover facts and details about your family the same must be recorded and saved. In addition to notes, over the years many different printed forms have been devised by other researchers who had the same organizational problems that you will encounter. Several of the most common forms are included in the Appendix at the end of this handbook, and nearly all genealogy associations, genealogical bookstores, and libraries have additional inexpensive forms for other family research uses.

Of the forms, perhaps the most often used is the *family unit chart* (also called a *family group sheet*, see Appendix 1), which focuses on an individual and his or her spouse and their children. These forms provide space in which to list numerous facts concerning their lives and those of their parents and children as well, all to be noted with the appropriate dates and sources. A three ring binder, such as may be procured in the school supply section of most any department store, is a convenient way to keep these and other forms. You should organize all forms in alphabetical order by *surname* (last name).

You should commence filling out and place in your binder a family unit chart for each and every marriage that you come upon. Also in the binder, and immediately following that family unit (or group) chart, you should have a sheet or two of lined paper for your future notes concerning the people within that family unit. This simple combination - along with the census forms mentioned below and included herein - will serve nearly all your organizational needs.

Also provided in Appendix 1 is what is called a *five generation pedigree chart*. It will provide an overall perspective of the last few generations of your family, from which vantage point you can move forward with your search. The pedigrees provide space for the minimum information concerning you, your parents, their parents, etc., back to and including your great-great grandparents. It is suggested that you now fill that form out as completely as possible. Remember however, even when the pedigree form is totally filled in, you will not have finished your research, you will have only commenced it. As said, genealogy is the study of family history, not a gathering of names and dates.

Of major importance are the forms for recording information gained from the various federal *Decennial Censuses*, again included in Appendix 1. As you will learn, censuses provide vital clues and data, and, as with all other information, your findings from these sources must be recorded in an understandable fashion.

Before you start, you should know that you will not find all of your people. Many ancestors will remain hidden for years, and some will never be uncovered. Know too that the frustration of being unable to link two people or to find a parent of some ancestor has been experienced by all who love this hobby. Still though, never decide that there is no point in looking further; as if by magic, ancestors sometimes appear when we least expect it. Now, as you commence and forever more, make a firm resolution that you will not guess and then presume a fact to be true; that you will not assume a kinship simply because it seems apparent and you have looked long and hard; that you will not represent to others that a relationship is likely if, in fact, you are not really sure yourself; and that you will not wish strange parents upon your ancestors. In short, if you are unable to prove a relationship, resolve now that you will not pretend, even to yourself, that you have done so.

ANCESTRY CHART

Maternal Family
Chart One

2 Lowell Carl MIDLAM
BORN 19 August 1903
WHERE Marion (Marion) OH
WHEN MARRIED 3 September 1927
DIED
WHERE

4 Carl Oscar MIDLAM
SPANISH-AMERICAN WAR -
service in Cuba

8 Oscar Washington MIDLAM
CIVIL WAR -
seventeen battles

16 Joseph MIDLAM   CONTINUED ON CHART

17 Martha Ann FREEBURN   CONTINUED ON CHART
                        Midlam-Freeburn 2

9 Phoebe Jane SHERWOOD
[Jennie]

18 Asa SHERWOOD   CONTINUED ON CHART
                                 Sherwood 2

19 Rebecca BROWN [Becky]   CONTINUED ON CHART
                         Brown-Meachem 2

5 Margaret Sophia HECKER

10 Jacob HECKER, M.D.

20 Jacob HECKER   CONTINUED ON CHART
                                  Hecker 2

21 Mary Eva   CONTINUED ON CHART

11 Anna Mary KRAUSE

22 Ferdinand KRAUSE   CONTINUED ON CHART

23 Sophia MOSIER (MOSHER)   CONTINUED ON CHART

1 Martha Ann MIDLAM [Martie]
BORN 18 September 1928
WHERE Marion (Marion) OH
WHEN MARRIED 15 April 1949
DIED
WHERE

NAME OF HUSBAND OR WIFE
Frederick Bedell ZIESENHEIM
3 September 1926
Erie (Erie) PA

Issue: Cydney Ann

3 Juliette Engle MORELAND
BORN 1 February 1906
WHERE Arthur (Moultrie) IL
DIED
WHERE

Issue: Martha Ann [Martie]
       Mary Lou
       Nancy Sue [Nancy]

Compiler: Martie Ziesenheim

6 Millard Hascal MORELAND
BORN 19 March 1877
WHERE Woodlawn, Shiloh Twp
(Jefferson) IL
WHEN MARRIED 29 October 1899
DIED 9 November 1964
WHERE (Marion) OH
Issue: Judson Orren
       Juliette Engle
       Millard Kirk

12 Judson R. MORELAND
BORN 22 April 1837
WHERE (Jackson) TN
WHEN MARRIED
DIED 14 November 1898
WHERE Woodlawn, Shiloh Twp
(Jefferson) IL

24 John? MORELAND   CONTINUED ON CHART

25   CONTINUED ON CHART

13 Juliette Jane DYCUS
BORN 5 December 1835
WHERE (Jackson) TN
DIED 17 May 1907
WHERE Ina (Jefferson) IL
-Odd Fellows Cem. Shiloh
Twp, with spouse

26 W. D. DYCUS (?)   CONTINUED ON CHART

27 Jane MILLARD? (?)   CONTINUED ON CHART

7 Nona Ethel KIRK [Nana]
BORN 1 January 1881
WHERE Spring Garden Twp
(Jefferson) IL
DIED 11 November 1968
WHERE Delaware (Delaware) OH
-Grand Prairie Cem.,
(Marion) OH, with spouse

14 William Franklin KIRK [Frank]
BORN 8 October 1855
WHERE Spring Garden Twp
(Jefferson) IL
WHEN MARRIED 1877
DIED 8 January 1932
WHERE Ina (Jefferson) IL

28 John L. KIRK [Jack]   CONTINUED ON CHART
                                   Kirk 2

29 Louise Anna SLINKARD   CONTINUED ON CHART
                          [Louisana -
                           Susannah]

15 Martha Ann Palestine SWEETIN
BORN 22 May 1858
WHERE (Franklin) IL
DIED 1929
WHERE Chicago (Cook) IL
-Kirk Cem., with spouse

30 Gilbert Grizell SWEETIN [G.G   CONTINUED ON CHART
                          Sweetin-Wyatt 2

31 Minerva Ann BROWN   CONTINUED ON CHART

A Five Generation Pedigree Chart

This is a nicely done, five generation pedigree chart. Notice that the
compiler provides the names of cemeteries, veterans' war service,
county names, and references to the charts that set forth the sixth and
further generations.

Evidence and Proof

Genealogy may be defined as the gathering, organization, consideration, and setting forth of facts and states of being concerning lineage. Accordingly, it is necessary that you now briefly consider the subject of evidence and proof.

You should carefully consider what tests and standards must be met before you may accept this or that accumulation of evidence as proof of some kinship. First off, always remember that speculation, interpolation, extrapolation, conjecture, and guesses are NOT evidence! Evidence consists of facts, states of being, and words. The existence of a gravestone is a fact, it and its total surroundings - its context - are a state of being, and the spoken or written materials concerning both are words. All three support numerous propositions and provide evidence to be interpreted by you. So too is a family tradition told to you by your grandmother, an entry in a Bible or newspaper, a war medal kept by a relative, or a recorded *deed* signed by an ancestor. Conversely, a guess or speculation by some cousin that an ancestor "must have" come from here or there because it makes "good sense" and he or she never heard anything different are NOT evidence and may not be used as proof of anything. Clues for future research, yes; evidence, no!

While the answers are not simple, the questions to be addressed in each instance of finding a new bit of evidence may be easily stated: Does this evidence speak directly to the question I am trying to answer, or, instead, is it but indirect evidence concerning that question? Should I rely on the source or should I look for a better and more reliable source of the same information? How much weight should be given this bit of factual material or, for that matter, any evidence learned from a source such as this one? Stated still another way, what is the value of this *evidentiary discovery*? A few examples will suffice for this study.

The genealogist has not been born who can state the value (or lack of it) of any bit of evidence without first knowing what it is that we seek to prove with that offering. All evidence varies greatly as to the weight it should be given (its *probative value*), depending entirely upon what question is being asked. Even a simple entry in an old family Bible varies greatly in its value depending on what we seek to prove with it. As an example, the name and date of birth of a child in a Bible probably is quite reliable as to the name of that child (usually that fact would be clear in the mind of one who undertook to write the entry), somewhat less reliable as to the precise date of the birth (the entry may have been written by other than a parent and probably was made some days or weeks later), even still less credible as to the importance of religion in that family (most everyone owned a Bible, then and now), and almost valueless in determining what became of that child in later life. So, to say flatly that Bible entries are reliable or not so is simply nonsense.

Then too, consider a military *discharge certificate*. It is almost surely reliable as to the name of the unit in which the soldier served, yet is almost valueless as it relates to the bravery of the soldier (even though, since he was honorably discharged, it is clear that he was not a total coward), equally lacking in value as to his attitudes toward war in general (many was the soldier who went to war only because he was required so to

Copy

Headquarters, Camp Chase,

Sept 1st ———— 1862

War Department
Adjutant General's Office
Washington August 20/62

Special Orders }
No 19 } (Extract)

10. The following officers having been ex
amined by a Board of Surgeons, and
found disabled, are hereby honorably
discharged the service.
Captain E. C. Francis 54th Ohio vols,
1st Lt A. J. Spaulding 32nd Ohio vols,
1st Lt Jno. E. Mobley 2nd Iowa vols,
2nd Lt R. W. Shoemaker 12th Ohio vols

By Order of Secretary of War
E. Townsend
Assistant Adjutant General

A true Copy

W. B. Allison
Col, Comdg Post

Military Discharge Certificate

If found physically unable to further serve, whether due to wounds or otherwise, many were discharged from service. In this document Captain E.C. Francis and Lts. A.J. Spaulding, J.E. Mobley and R.W. Shoemaker were so discharged.

do), and tells us virtually nothing as to the question of who were his parents or children. So, does the evidence before me speak directly to the question that I seek to answer, or to use this evidence must I *infer* something not here expressly written? The discharge expressly states the name of his military unit, yet I must infer his patriotism.

As another example, the simple existence of a headstone in a churchyard - that state of being - is almost proof positive that beneath lies a person of that name (notice, we said "almost"), somewhat less persuasive as to the dates contained on the stone (most likely that information was carved weeks, even months, after the death of the person buried there), still less reliable in any question as to the relationship of the deceased to others with the same surname buried nearby (especially if the name was a common one), surely quite unreliable if the question is whether or not the dead person attended services at that church (he may have died in a bar fight, for all we know, and was buried there through his mother's influence with the pastor), and is really nearly valueless if we seek to learn of the character or personality of that dead being (even though, still, we may make some tentative assumptions based on his presence in that geographical area). Remember too, that quite probably the deceased did not buy the headstone.

A family tale or tradition is often quite reliable concerning the names of the persons of whom it speaks and their locations at the time of the incident related, yet is very much less believable concerning the dates, numbers, and exact words of the participants. Books are only as reliable as were their authors, and are only quotable as authority and proof insofar as the author personally experienced the events or specified the original sources from which he gained the information set forth. If you would not be persuaded were the author speaking the words directly to you, then do not believe his writings. Note here that a novel, no matter how well researched and enjoyable to read, may not be quoted as proof of anything.

Many are the sources that must be used with caution and a generous measure of skepticism. Always look closely at the source of every fact or relationship, and earnestly ask yourself whether or not the evidence before you is the best available means by which to prove your point. If it is not, you must find the better source. Your genealogical research work is believable and has value only insofar as you have done a thorough job in seeking out and evaluating the best available evidence. A copy of a deed showing ownership is vastly more reliable (and believable) than a memory of a relative stating that same ownership. Your recollection of the given name of a grandfather is far less reliable than his mother's Bible entry stating that fact.

A word concerning sources from which evidence derives is appropriate. Some writers have needlessly undertaken to divide genealogical and historical materials into two categories; one they call *primary sources*, which category supposedly includes only those bits of evidence, artifacts, and writings that were done at or near the time of the event being recorded, or were written or performed by a person or persons who either was a participant or almost surely had knowledge concerning the subject matter, or both. The other category they call *secondary sources*. This latter grouping is said to include all evidentiary material that is derived, or abstracted, from or in some manner grows out of the primary materials. Though useless, such categorizations are easy in the extreme. It is apparent that we might label the handwritten dispatches of General Lee while he was at Gettysburg as "primary." Equally, someone's 1985 writings concerning Lincoln's thoughts at Antietam surely could be labeled as "secondary" under the definitions given. But how would we categorize a veteran's recollections written fifty years later concerning the heroic actions of another person who also was there? Obviously, we cannot. And if we could, to what purpose? Do we know any more or are we more able to use such facts because we label them?

So, we must examine ALL evidence, no matter how remote or from what source, and then decide either that we have proved our theory or that more evidentiary material must be gathered. A deed is probably more reliable than a newspaper entry showing the same ownership, yet both are evidence and both are vital to the researcher. A *birth certificate* signed by the attending physician (even though often containing errors) is likely more dependable than a Bible entry written some weeks after the birth, nevertheless both tend to establish that fact and must be carefully noted. An article in the Wall Street Journal relating that you were involved in a lawsuit is more reliable than a similar article in the gossip papers found at the supermarket check-out, yet is much less reliable than the record of the court clerk where the suit was filed. Whatever the measure of reliability might be in such a case, as a researcher you must gather and consider all such sources. Ignore all labels, and throughout the course of your searching examine all evidence, no matter how described by others. Make your decisions concerning reliability and the weight to be given data based solely upon your experience and sound judgment. *Genealogical proof* is nothing more (nor less) than the accumulation of that quantum of evidence - those bits of evidentiary material and facts - sufficient to convince a knowledgeable, diligent, and conscientious researcher that a relationship is established.

Measures of Evidence

"Convince" is the tricky word here, and what would convince one person might come nowhere close to doing so in the view of someone else. Because of that difficulty, genealogists (and historians) have long struggled with definitions, and the result has been to state that lineage must be proved by a *preponderance of evidence*, or that it must be of such a nature as to be *clear and convincing* to all. Despite those diligent efforts, both measures are so subjective as to be of almost no help, especially to the beginner.

So, how should you resolve the question? In the last analysis it is our intellectual honesty and integrity which control and demand that the accumulation of proof be of such clarity and forcefulness that the researcher need feel no embarrassment or lack of confidence in setting the findings forth before anyone in the intellectual community. Before lineage may be said to have been established there should be evidence of such weight and value that if nothing clearly to the contrary were presented a reasonable and intelligent person would consider the matter decided.

Enough of labels, evidence, and proof for now. The careful reader will learn as we go. So what do we do and where do we commence our search? There are three major categories of available sources. The first category is called by us *Interviews, Veterans, Churches, and Cemeteries.*

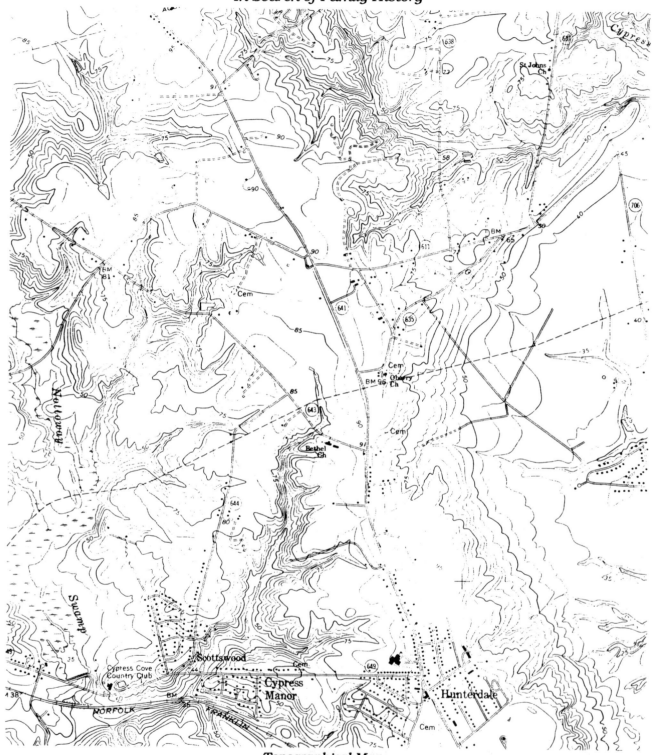

Topographical Map

Detail from the 1980, 7 1/2' Quadrangle for "Franklin, Virginia" by the United States Geological Survey. Note the precise detail of farm lanes, paved and unpaved roads, swamps, cemeteries, churches, schools, and houses and outbuildings. Such maps are of the utmost value to the family historian.

2

Interviews, Veterans, Churches
& Cemeteries

Living memories gained through interviews provide easily accessible facts and clues to myriad other facts, and most family researchers by no means have fully utilized the information that may be uncovered simply by questioning others. You must - repeat, MUST - talk to and gain all that may be learned from those relatives yet living who share common ancestors with you, especially the eldest ones. Countless times, a family researcher has gained a new fact from a member of another branch of the family whose recollections included information passed down through only their line. Remember that upon the death of such relatives their knowledge will be lost forever, and to uncover even a small part of what those folks have stored in their minds would take years of research. Indeed, most such facts could and would never be found.

So, you have arranged a meeting with a relative. Now what? Along with your three-ring binder and forms, if at all possible, take with you a tape or cassette recorder. As with the rest of us, your memory simply is not good enough to store all of the information you are about to gain. If a recorder is not available despite your best efforts, be prepared to write down ALL answers given, the same to be used for later comparison with your other notes. It also is very important that you take your camera, and if you have one, also take with you a map of the area.

The Importance of Maps

If you do not have a map, simply call or drop in at the office of the county engineer or of any surveyor in the area of your search. They will either have inexpensive maps or will direct you to someone locally who does. Then too, you might ask at the local Chamber of Commerce. Oftentimes they have area maps. Later, when you have established the precise neighborhood where an ancestor and his family made their home, you will want a more detailed map of that area. For that purpose, the best are the *U. S. Geological Survey 7 1/2' quadrangles*, called by most folks *topos* or *quads*. Such maps are inexpensive, very accurate and highly detailed, and show mountains, streams, swamps, vegetation, cities and towns, roads, rural houses and buildings, many cemeteries, notations of historical sites, and other information important to the genealogist. Often, the same county engineer, tax office, or Chamber of Commerce will stock such topos. If you already know the precise area you will need, and want to solve the map problem ahead of time, you may write to the U. S. Geological Survey, Washington, D. C., and ask for a list of 7 1/2' USGS quadrangles for those approximate areas in which you will be searching.

1844 WHEELER MAP OF PICKAWAY COUNTY
Madison Township

Location of the property in the township is designated by the letters indicated below, followed by the survey numbers.

N.W.—Northwest
N.C.—North Central
N.E.—Northeast
E.C.—East Central

S.E.—Southeast
S.C.—South Central
S.W.—Southwest
W.C.—West Central

C.—Central

* 1827 Landowners List.

Arndt, J. – S.W.   1/4 Sec. 33
Baum, C. – N.W.   1/4 Sec. 28
  N.E.   1/4 Sec. 29
Beery, D. – S.E.   1/8 Sec. 36
Bousher, I. – S.W.   1/4 Sec. 24
  N.E.   1/8 Sec. 24
Bowsier, J. – N.E.   1/8 Sec. 25
Boyer, – N.E.   1/8 Sec. 36
Brobst, D. – N.W.   1/4 Sec. 25
Brobst, J. – S.E.   1/4 Sec. 36
Brobst, P. – N.W.   1/8 Sec. 18
Case, M. – S.W.   1/8 Sec. 19
  N.W.   1/8 Sec. 32
* Cole, S. – N.W.   1/4 Sec. 13
Coon, G. – S.E.   1/8 Sec. 29
Crider, E. – S.E.   1/8 Sec. 25
Crist, A. – N.W.   1/4 Sec. 34
Culp, H. – N.W.   1/8 Sec. 19
Decker, J. & W. F. – S.E.   1/8 Sec. 19
  N.W.   1/4 Sec. 18
Decker, John – S.   1/2 Sec. 20
Decker, L. (heirs) – N.W.   1/8 Sec. 17
Decker, V. F. – S.E. 1/2 Sec. 20
  N.   1/2 Sec. 20
Dildine, H. – S.E.   1/8 Sec. 14
Duvall, B. – S.W.   1/4 Sec. 19
Feller, J. – N.W.   1/4 Sec. 35
Fisher, H. – S.W.   1/8 Sec. 31
Fisher, J. – N.   1/2 Sec. 31
Frankun, J. – S.E.   1/4 Sec. 34
Fridley, L. – S.E.   1/4 Sec. 25
Gibson, G. – S.W.   1/4 Sec. 32
Glick, D. – S.W.   1/4 Sec. 25
Glick, J. (heirs) – S.W.   1/4 Sec. 36
  N.E.   1/4 Sec. 27
Glick, S. – N.W.   1/4 Sec. 34
  N.E.   1/4 Sec. 27
  S.W.   1/4 Sec. 27
Hall, D. – S.W.   1/8 Sec. 36
Hall, L. – N.E.   1/4 Sec. 13
High, H. – N.W.   1/8 Sec. 19
Hines, J. – S.W.   1/4 Sec. 27
Hoover, A. M. – S.E. 1/4 Sec. 32
Huffines, I. – S.E. 1/4 Sec. 29
Kelly, J. – N.E.   1/8 Sec. 13
Keasel, J. – S.W.   1/4 Sec. 18
Kneffer, Jas. – N.E. 1/8 Sec. 26
Kneffer, Jno. – S.E. 1/4 Sec. 26
Kneffer, Jos. – W.   1/4 Sec. 26
Kiouse, D. – S.W.   1/4 Sec. 28
Knoninger, D. – E.   1/2 Sec. 34
Lambert, J. – S.W.   1/4 Sec. 14
Loffer, J. – N.E.   1/8 Sec. 19
Loffer, S. T. – N.W. 1/2 Sec. 23
Miller, I. – W.   1/4 Sec. 29
  N.W.   1/4 Sec. 32

Moore, C. A. – N.E.   1/8 Sec. 22
Noaker, J. – N.W.   1/4 Sec. 33
  S.E.   1/8 Sec. 33
Nothstine, J.
(Northstine) – N.W.   1/4 Sec. 13
  E.   1/2 Sec. 14
* Noyer, J. – S.E.   1/4 Sec. 24
  W.   3/8 Sec. 16
  S.W.   3/8 Sec. 21
  N.E.   1/8 Sec. 21
Perrill, A. L. (Parrill)
  W.
* Perrill, N. (Parrill) – S.W.   1/8 Sec. 15
  N.E. 1/4 Sec. 16   S.E. 1/8 Sec. 16
Peters, J. A. – S.W.   1/8 Sec. 31

* Rainer, A. (heirs) – N.E.   1/8 Sec. 17
* Rainer, D. (Rainer)
  N.W.
* Rarry, G. – N.   N.W.
  S.E. 1/8 Sec. 16   S. 1/2 Sec. 17
  N.W. 1/4 Sec. 17   N. 1/2 Sec. 15
Reeber, C. (heirs) – N.E.   1/4 Sec. 33
* Reed, G. (heirs) – S.E.   1/2 Sec. 30
Reed, R. (heirs) – W.   1/2 Sec. 30
* Ritter, J. – N.E.   1/4 Sec. 23
  N.W.   1/4 Sec. 24
Rose, A. – S.W.   1/8 Sec. 25

Sauser, J. – S.E.   1/4 Sec. 35
Schleik, S. – S.E.   1/8 Sec. 36
Shock, I. – S.W.   1/4 Sec. 15
Shock, P. – S.W.   1/8 Sec. 22
* Smith, J. – S.E.   1/8 Sec. 13
  S.W.   1/4 Sec. 23
Teagarden, A. – S.E.   1/8 Sec. 24
* Teagarden, D. – S.E. 1/4 Sec. 15
* Teagarden, J. – N.W. 1/4 Sec. 22
  N.E.   1/8 Sec. 21
* Teagarden, S. – S.E. 1/4 Sec. 22
Teagarden, W. – S.W.   1/4 Sec. 23
Toy, E. – S.E.   1/8 Sec. 21
  N.E.   1/4 Sec. 28
* Wilson, D. – S.E.   1/4 Sec. 31
Wilson, S. – S.E.   1/8 Sec. 19
Woolweaver, W. – N.E.   1/8 Sec. 14
* Wright, J. – E.   1/2 Sec. 18
Young, T. H. – N.E.   1/4 Sec. 27
Zwayer, J. – N.E.   1/8 Sec. 24

1844 Wheeler Map of Pickaway County
A reproduction of an excellent landowner's map of 1844, showing ownership of lands at that time.

Plan your visit and interview with the relative well ahead of time, all the while remembering that old folks tire easily, especially when called upon to think out and answer a long series of questions. So start with an easy question, and plan only to ask about a few important matters during the first interview session. Importantly: when you find that the person has tired, be polite; take a break or arrange a meeting at another time.

Sensitive Areas of Discussion

Since time immemorial, our people have had varying, yet usually quite steadfast and, to them, most appropriate views as to what they perceived to be matters of morality, especially concerning such subjects as adultery, illegitimacy, and divorce. By reason of such differing views, during an interview you may encounter a quite firm reluctance to continue with a certain topic under discussion. Good researchers do not press such matters; they search elsewhere.

Perhaps during an interview or in some other place, you will uncover a *black sheep* or two. When you do, remember that they are just as much a part of your family as are the upstanding citizens, and oftentimes are much more interesting. Further, as a family historian your task is to uncover, set forth, and preserve information, and good researchers never consider it their privilege to pass judgment upon the conduct or character of ancestors.

Commencing The Interview

As you start your interview with the relative, so too start a family unit chart (or family group sheet) for that person and his or her spouse, if there is or was one. As mentioned before, also be prepared to commence a family unit chart for all other marriages of which you learn in the course of that interview and every other.

Ask the relative to bring out old photos and mementos, not because you want to use them at that moment, because you don't (you will not know many of the people in the photos till after the interview), but because they will serve as valuable reminders for the person being interviewed. Be sure to utilize such keepsakes throughout your conversation. Incidentally, when you near the end of the interview, look again at those mementos and make sure you have knowledge of each of them, and be sure to ask to borrow those of significance in order that copies may be made for your records.

In the matter of your questioning, let us assume that the person being interviewed is your Aunt Jane, your mother's sister. Now, an interview is not an exchange of ideas, nor is it a debate. Let Aunt Jane do almost all of the talking. Listen carefully, and even if you believe that you already know the answers, ask the questions anyway. Until she tires, the more you ask the more you will jog her memory.

Ask all questions in terms of the relationships of the ancestors to the person being interviewed. Never ask questions in terms of the relationship of that ancestor to you. As examples, ask Aunt Jane "Who was your grandmother on your mother's side?"; Not, "Who was my maternal great grandmother?" (Note that they would be the same person.) "Did your grandmother live here in this county?" Not, "Where did my great grandmother live?"

So, remember to always inquire on the basis of the *kinship* of an ancestor to the person being questioned. After all, since you already know the relationship of Aunt Jane to you, after the interview you will be able to figure out how you tie in to the ancestor of whom you learned from Aunt Jane.

MONONCUE SCHOOL.

Report of *Maggie Carner*
for the month of *Feb.* 188*6*.

Days Present	17	Reading	85
Days Absent	3	Spelling	80
Deportment	85	Writing	
Arithmetic	50	U. S. History	6.
Grammar	80	General Average	
Geography	80		

J. H. Dundon Teacher.

Report of Maggie Carner
An early grade card revealing the place where Maggie Carner attended
school in 1885. She was 17 years old at the time.

Some - perhaps, indeed, the most important - clues to the records of the lives of ancestors are gained by the simple question, "Where did they live?" Often the answer is unknown to your interviewee, however by continuing to inquire as to past places of residence of other relatives - their brothers, sisters, cousins, etc. - you may well uncover the home place of the ancestor sought. So, if Aunt Jane does not know where her grandfather lived, ask "Do you remember any of your grandfather's brothers or sisters - your parent's aunts and uncles?" If she does recall her mother's old Uncle Bill, then ask

"Where did Uncle Bill live?" Her answer may be of value later, and it may also have been the same place where the missing parents lived. It is most critical to remember that if the recollections of the person being interviewed differ from your other notes, so be it! As mentioned, you are not there to argue, and often you will find that you are the one who is very wrong.

Techniques For Jogging the Memory

People often will provide you with answers that they did not think they knew. Example: if you simply ask Aunt Jane when her grandfather died, as likely as not she will say that she does not remember. Pursue the subject by asking if she was yet born or how old she was at the time of that death, whereupon you simply add or subtract that many years to or from her birth date and you have his approximate death year. Or you might ask if she and her husband were married when that grandfather died. If the answer is yes, then ask if any of her children had yet been born at the date of the death. The answer may be "Why yes, John was just a baby then. Still yet, we took him to the funeral. We drove the Model T, and it was so cold that day." By learning the birth date of that child, you then will know approximately when the ancestor died, and also that it was in the winter. All that, even though Aunt Jane had said that she did not remember. (You also know that they had a family car.)

Likewise, if she were to say "No, Jim was our middle child and wasn't born yet," thereby you will know that her grandfather died between the year of birth of her eldest child and the birth of Jim.

Just as women quite surely remember approximately how old a child was when this or that event occurred, men who lived in the 1920s, 1930s, and 1940s often recall what make and model of automobile they had at the time of important events; cars were much more important and significant in earlier days than now, and there were not nearly so many brands and names. Indeed, many present-day old men are able to recite a list of all the vehicles they have owned, and even the color of each. So, when told by an older man that he can not recall when an event took place, ask what make of car he then had or drove; it may well refresh his memory. When other memories of dates fail you might ask where the person being interviewed resided when the event occurred, then follow that question with an inquiry as to when they moved to or from that place. Quite usually a range of years will be gained thereby.

Finally, wars were (and are) long remembered and most important in the lives of all of us. The simple question, "Were any members of your family in a war?" often brings out many details not otherwise called to mind. If a date is not remembered, ask the person being interviewed if an event took place before the war recalled or before or after World War I or II, or the Korean, or Vietnam War. In summary, always relate your questions to dates, events, or residences that are or were then probably important or significant in the life of the person being interviewed.

Quite often, it is difficult for the person being interviewed to understand the precise nature of your interests. As an example, note that some certain second cousin of Aunt

Jane with whom she played as a child may be well remembered and most important to her memory, however the same cousin may be quite remote from your inquiry and of little interest to your present research. So, unless you already have developed an interest in the families of aunts, uncles, and cousins (which are known as *collateral branches* or *collateral lines*), it is important that you direct your questions only towards those branches of the family through which you are related to the person being interviewed, and in which you have particular interests. But, remember that notes should be kept of comments concerning those collateral lines, since in the future such knowledge may help you untangle family lines in which you have a greater interest.

Keeping Control Of The Interview

Then too, even though the conversation may move toward collateral lines in which you have little present interest, it is important occasionally to let the person being interviewed ramble. In so doing, they will relax just a bit and often will reveal facts about which you would not have thought to ask. Nevertheless, keep control of the interview, lest they stray too far from the purposes of your visit.

Additional Questions

In addition to asking where an ancestor and his family lived (especially if the interviewed person does not remember the answer to that question), try always to learn where the person being interviewed went when visiting elderly relatives, especially many years ago. Thereby, once again, new sources of records for future research will be revealed. Always ask the question, "Who is the oldest person you knew as a child?" In most families, there is someone who lived to be ninety (*nonagenarian*) or one hundred years old (*centenarian*), and through the *obituary* of that person you may learn many facts long forgotten by those now living.

Always note the date of the interview on the family unit chart. Often knowing when you learned a new fact will help later in evaluating conflicting information.

Always ask the person being interviewed if you may examine and study the notes in their family Bible, and then search through and copy all such notes precisely and thoroughly. Copy word-for-word even what you consider to be errors in spelling or mistaken dates. Remember, you very well may be the one who is wrong; we all have been.

Never fail to ask if there are any old letters, deeds, papers, or documents that you might read and copy (or keep). While there, be sure to take a photo of that relative, and have him or her hold a significant family heirloom. As soon as you can, preferably right then, and always, date the photographs.

Always seek to learn of family reunions that took place many years before. If there were any such events, seek diligently to learn when and where they were held in order that newspapers telling of the event later may be hunted down.

Southampton County Aug.t 26. 1873.

Dr William K. Drake ___

Dear sir, yours of the 12th inst.
came to hand 2 or 3 days ago. and I was glad to hear
that you were all in good health and blest with
good Crops; our crops have greatly improved during
the present month, so we all have cause for thank_
fulness and gratitude to the great Author of our exis_
tence for his loving kindness and mercies ;__ Enclosed
with this, you will find a letter to sister Drake from
her sister, I wrote the date on it by request :_ my know_
ledge about the best route for you and your brother to
come, is very limited, perhaps the one you have chosen
is the best ; ___ I hope you will be elected at the
coming election, I have long thought the Democratic
principles in ~~~~~~~~~ politicks was the best for
the whole Country. although I am aware, that I
know but little about it. __ I am about as I have
been for some time, hoping this will find you all well,
I shall look for a letter from you next month.

yours Respectfully
Tho. B. Worrell.

Old Letters and Correspondence
Much can be gleaned from even a short letter. Here, the writer revealed
his faith, that the recipient was then a "Dr." and was running for office
as a Democrat, that "sister Drake" had a true sister in old Virginia, and
that a visit there was contemplated by the recipient and his "brother."

Always ask if any ancestors are known to have used any words of a foreign language. If any did so, you then may have a clue as to when that branch of the family first came to this country and from where. Even though most families continued to speak the language of the old country for only one generation after arriving here, since the English language often had no words that could be substituted for items such as favorite food (bratwurst, baklava), expressions of anger and profanity (sacre damn), and other words not meant for the ears of children, old country words and expressions continued in use, often for several generations. Most of us long remember unusual expressions spoken by someone near to us, especially if spoken in a language other than English.

Then too, through foreign words - even those in a favorite recipe - one may gain a clue as to an area of prior residence. Even if they have no German lineage, few are the older women who do not have a recipe for a Pennsylvania Dutch dish if their grandmother or other close relative came from central Pennsylvania. Similarly, a family having a liking for grits or meat and biscuits for breakfast probably were influenced by persons from the South, and a taste for maple syrup probably came down from those of the northern states. So, even though pride in becoming American citizens led most folks to insist that their children learn and speak the language, a region or country of origin may arise from the speech of their descendants. But, remember that some nationalities, especially the northern Europeans, Greeks, and the Germans, clung stubbornly to both their past customs and their native language, oftentimes even for several generations.

Churches

What of churches and religious affiliations? They are extremely valuable sources of information! In the early days, virtually everyone went to church. They did so a) because they were God-fearing, b) because the law often required it, and c) by reason of the pleasure and social value of such meetings and gatherings. So be sure to ask about church affiliations of all ancestors mentioned or discussed. Draw the locations of such churches on your map, and whether or not those churches are still in existence drive out there, take pictures, and inquire of the pastors or other church officers as to the whereabouts of the birth, baptism, death, and other records of their congregation.

Records of such events as baptisms, deaths, confirmations, and even the meetings of early members often are still in existence, and at times such sources are most complete and incredibly helpful. Hence, if available to you, search those records very carefully. During that search, it is important to remember that nearly always the folks who were named as witnesses, sponsors, and participants in baptisms, christenings, confirmations, and dedications of children were relatives of the child - parents, aunts, uncles, grandparents, etc. Likewise, godparents usually were relatives. Remember that even if they were only friends, all such sponsors and participants had some relationship to the family, hence their presence provides clues for the careful researcher.

Note also that because there often were many children born to a family, christenings and baptisms were commonplace, and therefore the sponsors and witnesses at such events quite usually resided not far away. By reason of the time consumed and the

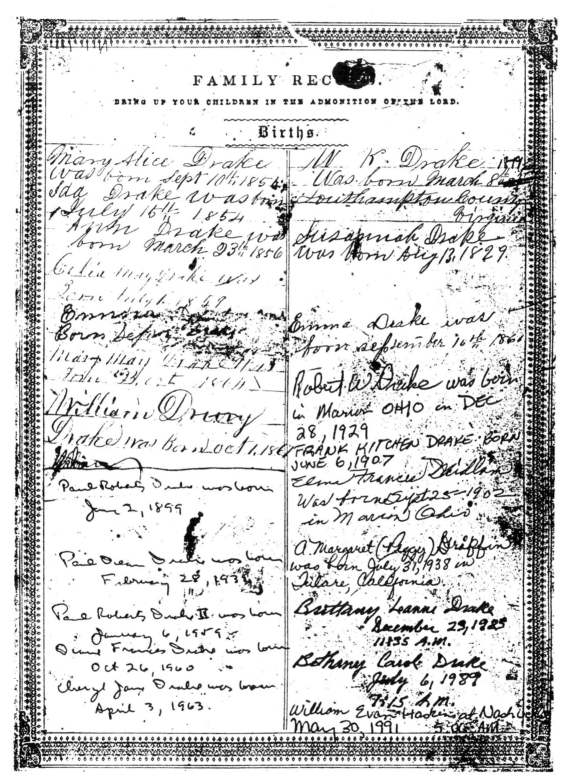

Family Bible, Births
Another page from a family Bible from 1850 that has been kept until now.

THOMAS R. ROBERTS CLAIMED BY DEATH

The Passing of Well-Known Resident of the City.

EXCELLENT CITIZEN HIGHLY ESTEEMED

Mr. Roberts Is Born in Wales, but Comes to This Country with Parents When Quite Young. Passes His Entire Life as a Farmer—Leaves Grown Family.

Thomas R. Robetrs, aged eighty-one years and eleven months, well known throughout the city and the county, died at his home, No. 502 north Prospect street, Saturday afternoon at 4 o'clock. Death was due to exhaustion, following an attack of grip and of pleurisy.

Mr. Roberts became ill six weeks ago. Up until that time he had been a remarkably well preserved man for his advanced years. He had lived in this county since 1872, coming here from Radnor township, Delaware county. He served as a member of the city council and was a Republican.

Mr. Roberts was born at Anglesey, North Wales, March 15, 1831, and came to the United States with his parents, who settled near Radnor, in 1837. He had twice been married, his second wife dying five years ago.

The deceased is survived by three daughters, all of whom reside in Marion. They are Mrs. T. E. Andrews, Mrs. W. D. Drake and Mrs. Guthrie Uncapher. He also leaves three brothers, William Roberts, of La Rue; Benjamin C. Roberts, of Richwood, and Edward Roberts, of Prospect.

A member of Kosciusko Lodge, No. 58, I. O. O. F., and all of the other local Odd Fellows bodies, Mr. Roberts, in spite of his advanced age, took an active interest in fraternal affairs. He was also a member of the Royal Arcaum.

Until he retired a number of years ago, Mr. Roberts had always followed his occupation of farming. He was one of the fine old men of the county.

The funeral services will be held at the late residence, Tuesday afternoon at 1 o'clock. Dr. Walter A. King, of the Trinity Baptist church, will officiate. Interment will be made in the Marion cemetery.

2 FEB. 1913

"UNCLE TOM" ROBERTS.

Obituary
A typical obituary column for a respected member of a community. Most obituaries were short and did not carry an etched likeness such as that found here.

difficulties of moving about on foot or by horse, folks normally did not travel long distances for such common-place events. Thus, the neighborhood or area in which an ancestor lived may be revealed by who was present at church events, common occurrences, and family gatherings.

If the old family church is no longer active, then visit a nearby church of the same denomination, and there inquire as to the whereabouts of the records (or even of the last record keeper) of the now inactive old congregation. When the records are not to be found locally, note carefully the name of and approximate year that activities in the old church ceased; you can use that information upon your next visit to the state capitol. Then, when at the *state capitol* and *archives* (of which later), inquire as to the location of any regional repository for that religious denomination. Two examples: in Nashville, Tennessee, you will find a substantial collection of materials and records pertaining to many early Baptist congregations, and the American Jewish Archives are located in Cincinnati, Ohio.

Likewise, and simply for the asking, there are available to us many other repositories of church records. Nearly always their collections are open to the public and are free. Incidentally, in the early days the best records were kept by the Quakers, Lutherans, and the Catholics, to which list, after about 1840, one may add the Mormons. Remember too that Orders of Sisters (nuns) often owned and operated schools, and their valuable records of students sometimes may be uncovered simply by inquiring of the local parish priest.

Cemeteries

Finally, and very importantly, many churches maintained cemeteries, the records for which are often kept locally with the other church documents. So, inquire of the pastors, clerks, or members of the congregation concerning such facilities and records.

Always ask Aunt Jane for the names and locations of ALL other cemeteries wherein family members are thought to be buried, and carefully locate them on your map. Much will be learned by your visits there. Note too that most cemeteries - even the smallest ones - have formal or informal names, e.g., "Bishop Cemetery", "Pleasant Hill Cemetery", etc. Make a note on the family unit chart of any such names for use in your later inquiries in that area or in cemetery lists.

Since walking horses and mourning people move at only about three miles an hour, ancestors nearly always were buried within three or four miles of their homes, and, just as now, very few persons were buried off by themselves. So, the locations of graves usually indicate that the dead lived nearby, and graves which are close to those of your ancestors very well may be those of relatives. Note all information found on every family grave marker, and make notes of the dates and names found on the headstones immediately surrounding those graves. As suggested above, if the cemetery once was a churchyard inquire of folks living nearby as to the name and denomination of that old church, that information to be used later when visiting the church record repositories or the archives.

~❧Funeral Notice❧~

Died, on Sunday morning, May 18, 1890, at 4 o'clock,

Mrs. Martha Midlam,

Wife of Joseph Midlam, aged 92 years, 2 months and 20 days.

The·FUNERAL·SERVICES

Will be held at the Evangelical Church, this city, Tuesday, May 20th, at 2 o'clock, p m., and will be conducted by Rev. D. H. Wonder.

Interment at the Mission Cemetery.

Friends of the family are invited to attend.

A Funeral Notice
By the 1890's, funeral notices, sometimes called "mourning cards," were in common use. Due to advances in printing, undertakers, even in small communities, could produce them in a day. Many examples can still be found in family collections.

Remember that most headstones deteriorate in a few score years, and within your lifetime grave markers that are now difficult to read will be illegible and lost forever. So, take photos of all family headstones and carefully preserve a record of what is written on each. If the carving in the stone is difficult to read, often the problem may be solved by brushing away the dirt and debris with a soft bristle brush (not metal), then placing thin brown wrapping or meat paper tightly over the stone, and thoroughly rubbing red or blue carpenters' chalk (available in every hardware store) or dark crayons over the paper.

Another easy way is to spray the stone with ordinary shaving cream, and then quickly wipe over it with a squeegee such as is used to clean windows. For a few seconds the old writing often will be quite visible..

In early times, particularly in the tidewater counties of the colonies from Maryland south, there was no native stone from which to make cemetery markers, and only the wealthy or nearly so had the means to have such stone shipped from the other colonies. For those reasons, many of your southern ancestors were buried without markers other than those made of wood which are now long turned to dust. Then too, even in those settled areas where stone was available merely for the taking, stone carvers either had not yet arrived or charged unaffordable fees for their services. So it was that very often the men of the family made monuments to the dead with a piece of ordinary field stone and a 'cold chisel', often inscribing only the initials. Nevertheless, even these sometimes are rendered legible by the use of chalk or shaving cream.

If the cemetery has an office and record keeper (called a *sexton*), ask if you may search the *Index to Interments*. Check it for all persons who had the surnames you are searching. Do so, even if you think they are not related. If there is no cemetery office, ask a neighbor for the name of the caretaker, grounds keeper, or person who mows the grass, and then inquire of him or her. Such folks often know many very important details concerning families buried there and of others like you who have visited and inquired after specific families and names. Mowing a cemetery time after time lends a considerable depth of knowledge, hence such folks often will know quite positively if a family name is not familiar to them, thus saving you much time and also revealing that you probably are in the wrong place.

As mentioned, be sure to ask the caretaker if others have inquired after the same graves or surnames. If they have, you may establish a most valuable research friend, relative, or family line. Some cemeteries even have log books or journals in which researchers record their names, addresses, and the names of the deceased for whom they are searching. You should sign it too.

Back to the interview. Of very great importance are family traditions and favorite tales and stories. Remember, that while the details of such stories usually are often quite unreliable, such tales almost invariably contain elements and a core of truth, which facts will provide very valuable clues for future research. So, inquire about traditions and, as always, make complete notes, even if the stories are fanciful.

Veterans

Always ask, especially, if there are stories or tales concerning wars in which members of the family fought or were otherwise involved. As with family traditions, war stories often carry down through a family for numerous generations. Why search out military records? Two reasons: 1) You probably will be very proud of that ancestral service, and 2) the records of veterans provide much information not to be found anywhere else.

A few words about war are important to your understanding. In early times, especially before the Civil War, there seldom was a *draft* - conscription - as we know it. Most men enlisted only when the war came to the neighborhood or when they otherwise perceived that their family was in danger, and were discharged in a very informal fashion when the fighting moved off to another place. So it was that men generally voluntarily joined organizations or units being formed close to where they lived. Hence, if you learn of a Revolutionary or War of 1812 ancestor who joined the army at Reading, Pennsylvania, you have an excellent clue as to his place of residence at the time of that enlistment. The likelihood that a veteran lived close to his place of enlistment or conscription exists even now; we still usually go to the local office to enlist and are drafted from the local area.

Be sure to ask where the person being interviewed believes a certain veteran to have lived; he or she may know, and so save you the search. At least try to learn of the area or region from which that ancestor is thought to have come, and, especially in the case of the Civil War, ask for what side he or she served or fought.

One old Tennessee mountain man related that his grandfather (whose name he did not recall) had been "...marched off by them soldiers and never heard of again." When asked in what war that incident took place, he replied, "Back there when the Democrats fought the Republicans." He was referring to the Civil War, of course. Having later learned of the whereabouts of the home of that grandfather at the time of the war, it was possible for the researcher to learn his name, what Confederate unit had taken him away, and even to where.

The National Archives and Veterans' Records

The available records vary from war to war, and to a considerable extent (even for the early wars) such records are still in existence, copies of which may be procured through the *National Archives* (see also Appendix 2). Simply write to the General Reference Branch (NNRG-P), National Archives and Records Administration, 7th and Pennsylvania Avenues, Washington, D.C. 20408, and request six or so sets of *Form NATF-80*, which are free of charge. You must use these forms to obtain copies of the records of veterans, as simple letters of request and inquiry are not acceptable at the Archives.

For the wars up to and including the Indian wars of the late nineteenth century three categories of records usually were retained. They are a) those that concern the military movements and activities of the veteran, b) those that pertain to his *pension application* and the terms of the pension itself (whether or not he ultimately received one), and c) those which have to do with service connected *land grants*, i.e., the *bounty land records*, again, whether or not it was ultimately determined that he really had any such rights.

So, if you want all categories searched (and you surely do), complete NATF-80 forms for each category you want searched as fully as possible for each veteran, and then return the forms to the Archives. If you also desire the records of widow's pensions and benefits, NATF-80 forms must be submitted for them too. Unlike for veterans, for widows you will need only one form since almost always they performed no military service.

The forms are easy to fill out. Note, though, that Archives employees are busy, hence it is wise to order the blank forms now in order that you may have them on hand when you need them in the future. Upon receipt by the Archives of your completed NATF-80s, the folks there will do the records search for that ancestor, and if he or she is found in any of the categories mentioned, you will be notified that the records have been located. Thereupon, you will have thirty days within which to forward the nominal fee designated for copies of those records. Usually, $10.00 is now required for each category of records found. When sending in the forms, be sure to tell them that you want copies of all the papers in the file, otherwise sometimes they will select what they think appropriate and important, and you may not be sent all the available information.

Concerning the bounty land records, note that commencing in colonial times, and especially after the American Revolution and continuing through the Indian wars, nearly until the twentieth century, land usually was granted as one of the rewards for military service. Thereby, as with other inexpensive land settlement programs, the veterans were encouraged to take their families and clear and settle portions of the vast wilderness that yet remained. In fact, grants of land to veterans continued through the nineteenth century (1800s), and homesteading sponsored by both the States of the Union and the Federal government took place in Alaska down through the 1970s. Homesteading was even attempted by the State of Minnesota as recent as 1988, albeit unsuccessfully. All such governmental efforts to encourage settlement resulted in records and record keeping that will have great value to you.

Moreover, throughout nearly all of our history, pensions and other benefits have been granted to those who served the nation in times of war. Then, after the deaths of those veterans, certain of those benefits also were granted to their survivors, especially their widows. The claims for all such benefits resulted in records valuable to the family historian.

Since, as noted, the methods used for recruiting and discharging our early volunteer veterans usually were quite informal, very often little or no record was kept by the government of the wartime activities of individual soldiers or even of their military units. Accordingly, later it often was impossible from the records alone to determine who should receive pensions, land, and other benefits, and who should not. So it was that after being placed under oath, the veterans (and their dependents or widows) who sought such rewards were required to give complete statements of those facts which rendered them eligible. In these sworn statements quite often were listed the parents of the veterans; their birthplaces and ages; their residencies before, during, and after the wars; marital status and the names of their wives; the names of dependents, brothers, and sisters; as well as the units in which they served, the battles in which they participated, and other wartime activities. Such records are often genealogical gold mines.

Concerning veterans' records, it is very important to remember that until the year 1818, only those Revolutionary veterans who were maimed and disabled were awarded pensions. Then from 1818 until 1828, in order to qualify for a pension, a veteran had to demonstrate very reduced means - poverty. That latter requirement resulted in *affidavits* and lists setting forth the total belongings owned by the veteran, which lists are delights to read. Then, after 1828 all of the still surviving veterans were pensioned. Finally, in 1836 widows of veterans also were granted monthly pensions.

Notice then, because of those changing requirements many men who served in the Revolution received no pensions whatever, and so often escape detection by the researcher. Why? Because if a Revolutionary veteran died BEFORE 1818 and was NOT maimed or disabled during service, or if he died BETWEEN 1818 and 1828 (between thirty-five and forty-five years after the end of the war) and was neither poverty stricken nor maimed, his name will not appear in the pension records, even though his widow might later appear.

So, where then will he be revealed? He likely will be found within the land records, since his rights to land grants or to receive warrants that could be traded for land or sold, as the veteran chose, were not dependent upon his age, physical infirmity, or financial condition. So it is that the land warrant records may be the only evidence of his service that the researcher will find in the National Archives.

A word as to bounty land warrants and grants: in the early days (as now) the Federal government owned vast quantities of raw and undeveloped land. The warrants - vouchers of sorts, legal documents - awarded to veterans, others who had served the nation, and often ordinary citizens as well, could be exchanged for land at the land offices established for each area, territory, or group of territories. (As we shall see, the states also frequently owned land and made grants to their veterans in like fashion.) Each warrant set forth the quantity of land to which that person was entitled, depending upon the established value of his or her rank or services. Then, generally speaking, even though there were many variations, upon arrival at the land office the veteran shopped through the list of available tracts of that quantity, selected the tract he wanted, had it surveyed (if necessary), and then, upon return of the survey showing no encroachment upon the lands of others, received the grant - the original deed - to that tract. That grant was written on very fine paper or *vellum* (calf, lamb, or kid skin) and while usually issued by the land offices and bearing their seals, sometimes were signed by the President who caused the *Great Seal Of The United States* to be affixed. The grant then was recorded in the courthouse of the territory or state where the land was situated, copies of many of which, as we shall see, may still be procured (see page 30).

Caution: since, as mentioned, land warrants owned by a veteran had value and legally could be sold by him, often they were. Further, such warrants sometimes were

6366

Pennsylvania

Catherine Carner, dec'd. late,
widow of

Anthony Carner, deceased
who was a pensioner under the Act of 1818.
and who died on the 17 June 1834
of Centre Co in the State of *Pennsylvania*
who was a Sergeant in the Compy commanded
by Captain Thompson of the regt commanded
by Col Clark on the N. Carolina
line for 2 years

Inscribed on the Roll of *Pennsylvania*
at the rate of 120 Dollars ---- Cents per annum,
to commence on the 4th day of March, 1836 ending
31st " " " 1840

Certificate of Pension issued the 11 day of Sept
1841 & Sent to Geo. Buchanan Esqr.
Bellefonte Pennsylvania

Arrears to the 4th March 40 $480.00

Semiannual allowance ending 31st
March 40 the day of her death $9.00

$489.00

{ Act July 7, }
{ 1838. }

Recorded by Theo L. Moody **Clerk,**
Book a **Vol.** 2 **Page** 148
Payable to children of said deceased viz
William & John Carner & Julia Geary —

Widow's Pensions

Here is a portion of the record of Catherine Carner's "Widow's Pension"
#6366 as found in the National Archives, and procured from there
through use of the form NATF-80.

No. 163.159

APPROPRIATION.

Bounty Act July 11 1862,   75.

Payroll Rolls.   23.75 —

$98.75 —

TREASURY DEPARTMENT,

SECOND AUDITOR'S OFFICE,

April 29 , 186 5

I certify, That I have examined and adjusted the claim of

John E. McCann decd *Pri D 13 Cav. Trimble*

and find there is due *him* from the United States the sum of *Ninety Eight*

dollars and ___ *75* ___ cents, being for

Pay &c from Mar 1st to June 27 1864 & the
Bounty of $ 100. under Act July 22 1861.

as appears by the account and vouchers herewith transmitted for the decision of the Second Comptroller of the Treasury thereon. To be paid to *William W. McCann Father of*

deceased or *his* order, by any Paymaster of the Army, in the
district of the claimant's residence. *Tenn.*

E. B. French

Second Auditor.

Second Comptroller's Office,

$98.75

May 6 , 186 5

The above claim of *ninety-eight*

dollars and *75* cents is admitted.

Second Comptroller.

[Should this Certificate be assigned, the blanks for date and the Paymaster's name will not be filled until the Certificate is taken up as a voucher by a Paymaster.

The blank for the amount will be filled at time of transfer and the receipt signed by the present holder. The form for transfer on the back of the receipt will be filled with the name of the person to whom transferred and signed by the same person who signs the receipt in the presence of two witnesses. All these signatures to the assignment will be made before and attested by a Notary Public or Justice of the Peace—the officer before whom the original affidavit of applicant for arrears of pay was made, if possible.]

Received this *third* day of *August* , 186 5.

from *L. T. Thistle* Paymaster *Ninety eight* —

dollars *Seventy five* cents, in full of the above

Witnessed by—

Geo. R. Adrian

James N. Craig

William W. McCann

"Bounty" Money

A copy of an original record showing $100.00 "bounty" money paid to William McCann by reason of the Civil War death of his son, John McCann. Such information can, again, be procured from the National Archives through the use of Form NATF-80.

converted into land, whereupon the land itself was sold. So, land warrants, or the unsettled land resulting from such warrants, may never have provided a residence for a veteran ancestor. Indeed, he may never even have seen the property. Accordingly, you must not presume that an ancestor lived on a tract simply because he had a warrant for it, or because he once owned it.

On the other hand, many a soldier was granted wilderness land, cleared it, built a house, raised a family, lived out his life, and found his final resting place there. So, be very careful in making assumptions based on land warrants found in the names of your ancestors.

In summary, unless you know when a veteran died and have knowledge of his physical condition and economic status, it is well to seek out all forms of records mentioned - land warrants and the pension and military activities files. Remember, any veteran not maimed, who also was not poverty stricken, and who did not live to extreme age, likely died without ever appearing in the pension records. But also remember that if his widow was alive after 1836, she may appear in those very records even though he did not, and her pension application and file will be every bit as complete as his would have been. Indeed, from the standpoint of genealogical information to be gained, widows' records often are more informative than are those of the veteran since a widow's claim rested entirely upon kinship to the veteran and not upon her military service, and so required proof of marriage, sworn statements concerning residences, children, etc.

Veterans' Records in Libraries

It also is important to note that during and after wars, particularly the Revolution and the War of 1812, the States of the Union and the U.S. Government quite usually permitted citizens to file claims for property destroyed by acts of war and for non-military services rendered or supplies furnished by them to the armed forces. Thereby will be revealed the locations or residences of ancestors, thus leading the researcher to the libraries and courthouses of that area. The many such claims have been the subject of articles and books which can be found in nearly all large libraries and state archives.

It also is very important to remember that not all existing veterans' records (especially those of the Revolution and War of 1812) are housed in the National Archives. Many was the soldier who served in combat with a unit of a state *militia*, rather than in any national military unit. Such militia records very often were retained only in states' archives. Then too, as suggested above, many states had undeveloped land to grant as rewards for services. Accordingly, if you do not find an ancestor in the national records, yet by reason of his having been of military age you suspect that he did serve, you must search the records of those states and colonies which either existed or were carved out of those that did exist at the time of the war being researched.

When searching for Revolutionary ancestors and their families, keep in mind that most large libraries have very fine indexes to the records of the *Society of Daughters of the American Revolution (D.A.R.)*, which contain thousands of names of patriot veterans, as well as the names of myriad descendants who, by reason of the service of their ancestors, are now or were once affiliated with that organization or sought to be so associated. The magnificent library of the D.A.R. is in Washington, D.C., and is open to the public. So too is the fine library of the *Society of Sons of the American Revolution (S.A.R.)* located in Louisville, Kentucky. Again though, remember that those records do not contain the names of every single veteran.

If you find that an ancestor was a veteran of the Revolution, you are eligible to be considered for membership in either the D.A.R. or in the S.A.R. Further, there are many other organizations for which you may be eligible as a result of the military service of an ancestor in that and other later wars.

List of Officers for 1906

Post Commander	B. W. Kerfoot
	18 Logan Street
Sr. Vice Commander	F. W. Ritter
Jr. Vice Commander	W. J. Pasco
Adjutant	A. J. Smith
	209 Linden Avenue
Quartermaster	Ns D. Bates
	30 McDaniel Street
Surgeon	E. L. Hill
Chaplain	A. S. Jones
Officer of the Day	E. Middleton
Officer of the Guard	H. S. Rockey
Sergeant Major	Albert L. Davis
Quartermaster Sergeant	W. H. Pritz
Inside Sentinel	Wm. J. Kinsella
Outside Sentinel	J. G. Miller

TRUSTEES

John Deis,　　J. C. Cline,　　T. C. Lindsey

ROSTER
...of...
The Old Guard Post No. 23
Department of Ohio, G. A. R.
Dayton, Ohio, January 1, 1906.

Membership 446.

Those not otherwise designated belonged to Volunteer Infantry Regiments.

Anderton, Charles, Corp. A, 93 O.   356 Arcade Bldg.
Atwood, Henry, Sergt. H, 100 N. Y. I.   108 E. Center
Ambrose, James A., B, 4 Bat. O. Cav   134 Jones
Allan, Eban S., G, 131 O.   717 E. Richard
Arnet, W. H. H., Q. M. Sergt. 5 O. Lt. Art   254 Newcom
Allison, John G., G, 14 Mo.   N. S. Oxford Ave.,
                W. of Chester Ave.
Austin, C. C., G, 154 O.   18 Sycamore
Arnold, H. J., K, 63 O. V. I.   W. Milton

Bates, Ns Doren, Sergt. G, 67 Ind. I   39 N. McDaniel
Brusman, Lafayette, G, 65 O.   621 N. Main
Bates, Wm. L., Corp. A, 131   553 W. Second
Beck, J. S., Q. M. Sergt. 90 O.   38 W. Fifth
Bell, John N., Capt. E, 25 Iowa I   322 S. Jefferson
Brandt, Wm. F., A, 4 O. C.   730 E. Richard
Buvinger, E. E., B, 4 O. C. & A. 131   68 E. Green
Buvinger, Geo. W., B, 4 O. C. A. 131   29 E. Marshall
Birch, John, 2 Lieut. K, 22 O. & C. 1 O. 108 N. Floral ave
Blum, John, I, 19 O.   411 Jackson
Bain, James E., F, 34 O.   254 W. Lafayette
Bennett, John K., I, 1 O Cav   260 N. Valley
Bonbright, Dan., 1st Lieut. E, 11 Pa., 125 S. Western ave
Boyer, E. C., A, 131 O.   2234 E. Fifth
Brush, James W., B, 81 O.   110 N. St. Clair
Barlow, Jno. T., Corp. I, 11 O. Rooms s. e. c. First & Main
Bussard, Wm. H., Musician, H, 35 O   78 E. Jones
Bradstreet, J. M., C, 35 O.   318 W. Fifth
Bradstreet, W. H., Band, 35 O.   332 W. Monument ave
Buxton, John M., Corp. H, 33 N. J. I.   Mil. Home

1

G.A.R. Roster Booklet
An often found roster booklet of a G.A.R. Post. The vast majority of Civil War veterans were in the Grand Army of the Republic (G.A.R.) or its counterpart, the United Confederate Veterans (U.C.V.). The records of their local organizations are often found in the states' archives and are very valuable sources of information.

Societies and Clubs

Speaking of societies, since the earliest times, and in this country especially since the middle of the nineteenth century (1800s), men and women have sought to be members of societies (patriotic and otherwise), clubs, organizations, sororities, and fraternities. Thus, it is quite likely that one or more of your ancestors will be found to have so belonged. The *Order Of The Cincinnati, United Daughters of the Confederacy, Rebekah Lodge, The Sons of Union Veterans, Sons Of The Revolution* (to be distinguished from the S.A.R.), *Colonial Dames*, the *Eastern Star, Masons, Shrine, Order of Red Men, Woodmen of the World, Odd Fellows, Moose*, and the *Elks* are but a few of the very many. By contacting the local secretary of those organizations (try the telephone directory), or by inquiring at the state archives concerning now defunct societies, you may uncover records of memberships, which often reveal ages, dependents, marriage dates, and other interesting and important facts no where else to be found.

After you have completed the interviews, obtained the veterans' records, visited the churches and cemeteries, and assembled, recorded, and organized the information obtained from those sources, you are ready to go to the libraries.

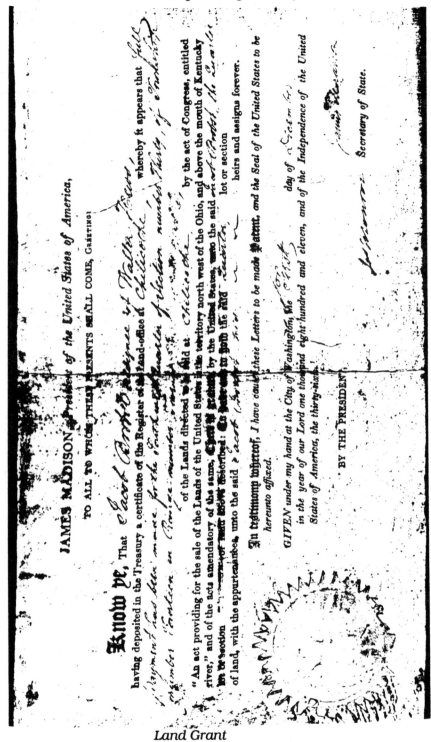

Land Grant

This very rare land grant is on vellum and was signed in 1811 by President James Madison and his then Secretary of State, James Monroe (who later became president as well). The document bears the Great Seal of the United States and granted land located near Lancaster, Ohio, to Revolutionary War veteran Walter Hews (Hughes) who assigned the rights to one Jacob Brobst. A true genealogical treasure.

3

Libraries

In large part, family research is a search of *indexes*, and libraries have plenty of these. Most of us do not have direct access to the giant libraries and renowned collections of genealogical materials, of which there are several. The *Library of the Church of Jesus Christ of Latter Day Saints* (*LDS* or *Mormon Library*) in Salt Lake City, Utah; the *Public Library of Allen County* in Fort Wayne, Indiana; and the collection in the *Library of the City of New York* perhaps are the best known and largest of the great American sources. Further, all state capitols and most large cities have substantial collections, especially concerning that state, the surrounding area, and many of those areas from which local peoples migrated. All are available for your careful use and usually are free. Smaller, nevertheless equally important to you, are the numerous collections dedicated to special groups such as German immigrants, Baptists, physicians, members of the armed forces, etc., and, of the utmost significance, those collections found in nearly every local library.

Commencing Your Library Research

To commence your library research, walk in and ask the librarian to direct you to the family history (genealogy) section and to the genealogy *catalog*. The genealogy catalog may be with the main catalog or may be by itself, and may be either in card form or computerized, or both. If the catalog is on computer, do not be intimidated. Read the instructions, and ask for help if you do not understand.

Always remember, however, that librarians are not there to do your research, nor do they have time to listen to long stories about your family, no matter how interesting such tales may seem to you. In short, while the library folks will be happy to help in many ways and to direct you to materials which are available for that county and area, you have to do the work; they will help you locate the books you need, but you have to do the reading.

Changing Boundaries

To do good library research, you must make some adjustments in your thinking. Today, the states of the Union are quite usually divided into well established cities, towns and counties, the last in turn divided into townships or districts, townships into precincts, etc. While we are accustomed to the unchanging nature of the boundaries of such *political subdivisions*, that was not always the way of things. As a result, one of the most common shortcomings of the newcomer to family research is the failure to realize

31

that nearly every political division had its beginnings as a part of another one or more larger and different townships, counties, states, or territories. Note too that while their boundaries frequently change, cities and towns also may be divided into wards and precincts.

All of our present states and territories underwent such changes. As an example: nearly all of what now is Ohio, Indiana, Illinois, Michigan, Wisconsin, and Minnesota was a part of New France until the conclusion of the French and Indian War, after which those lands became English. They then became part of the Northwest Territory and soon after the American Revolution were governed largely by the Ordinance of 1787. Later - in 1803 - the part of that territory now called Ohio was admitted to the Union as a state and was, then, divided into six counties, some reserved Indian lands, and a military district set off as a source of lands for veterans, etc. By 1820 - its counties all the while being divided into townships, sections, etc. - Ohio had been further subdivided into sixty-two counties, and, finally, by 1860, as today, there were eighty-eight (88) counties, all divided into townships as their individual needs varied and demanded. (Note here also that what you know as counties and townships may elsewhere, now and in times past, be called precincts or manors or even towns.)

In addition to the changes themselves, the reasons for such changes are important to the researcher. Over a period of now some three centuries, as land was gained from France, Russia, Spain, and the Indians, our settlements have continually moved west and south, generally. Indeed, such was the state of affairs until virtually all of the land between the oceans and between Canada and Mexico was settled and had become a part of our nation. Further, even as each new county and state was being established, land seeking pioneers already were moving outward and away from the newest settlements.

As people moved, so did their government. Just as before they migrated to the new settlements, the outermost of the settlers had to have continuing access:
    a) to those offices established for the preservation of documents and other evidence, particularly concerning land transactions and death (land grants, deeds, leases, mortgages, records of veterans, and wills and estates);
    b) to the law, which, it was hoped, would protect such rights and privileges (courts, judges, and law enforcement officers such as sheriffs, constables, and justices of the peace); and
    c) to a place positive from which taxes could be assessed and to which the same might be paid, the last mentioned surely more desired by the governing bodies and officials than by the settlers.

The place where those offices and facilities were located quite usually was (and is) called the *county seat*, so called since that was the seat of government; that place where officials literally sat and conducted the affairs of the public and common good.

In early times, much more so than now, the need to remain at home to tend to and protect their families, farms, and livelihoods, brought the belief and virtual requirement that not more than a single day of travel should be required to attend to government business. As a result, even though a distinct minority frequently traveled about for reasons of commerce and land activities, most of our farming pioneer ancestors were reluctant to leave home for any period of time. Thus, the more distant the county seats were from those farmers, the less accessible government was.

Since nearly all travel had to be on foot, on horseback, or in small boats, the distance between county seats ended up being not much more than about thirty miles (except in the great prairie states where the cattle grazing business required much larger boundaries). So it was that as soon as the outermost settlers were thirty, forty, or so miles distant, and the landholders and their lands were sufficient in voice, number, and tax dollar value to justify the formation of such, another county was formed. Each new county was given a name and almost always was assigned quite specific boundaries.

So, why are these historical facts and reasons important to the family researcher? Because, by reason of the continuing changes in county names and boundaries, a frontier farmer might settle, build a home, raise a family, never move, and yet over his lifetime be a resident of several different townships, counties, and even of different states of the Union. You must remain constantly conscious of that likelihood if you are to adequately research the lives of your ancestors.

Examples? There are many. Suppose you find that an ancestor and his family lived in Cumberland County, Pennsylvania, in 1770. Then you find that in 1776 they were no longer listed there yet when you happen to search the Bedford County tax lists you find them again. Thereafter, in 1787, they disappear from the Bedford records, however they then turn up in the records of Huntingdon County. They sure moved around a lot, didn't they? To the contrary, perhaps not at all. Perhaps not even once!

You see, part of old Cumberland County was carved away to form Bedford County in 1771, and following that (in 1787) Bedford provided the land from which was formed Huntingdon. Thus your people could have settled on land in Cumberland County after the Indian title was extinguished in 1760, lived and raised their families there over the following thirty years - as many did - and casually looked on and went about their business while their land became, first, a part of Bedford, and then, seventeen years later, a part of the new Huntingdon County.

Moreover, suppose that ancestor died on the home place and left it to a son who, with his family, continued to live there until his death in 1850. In 1846, Huntingdon too was carved into two parts; one remained Huntingdon, but the other part became the new Blair County. So, if your ancestral farm was in that part of the old Indian land which ultimately became Blair County, you would find the estate records of that son and his family in the Blair courthouse. Over a period of but ninety years the family would have lived in four distinct governmental entities and yet not have moved even once. Thus, as you move backward through the years, to keep track of just that single family you would be called upon to seek out the records in the courthouses for Blair, Huntingdon, Bedford, and Cumberland counties.

Other examples are too numerous to mention, however notice that Bourbon County, of what is now Kentucky but once was Virginia, contributed a portion of its territory to

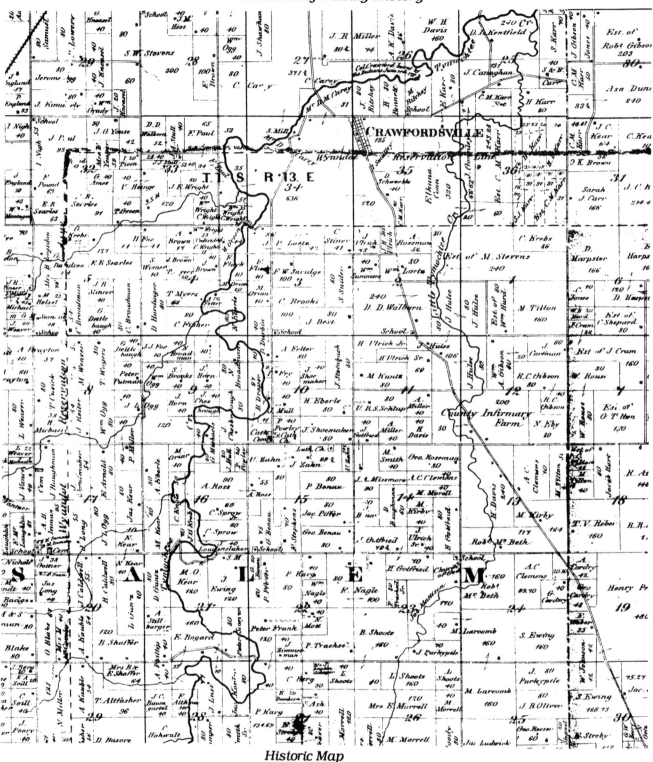

Historic Map

This map, a most valuable reproduction, shows Salem township of Wyandot County, Ohio, and its recorded landowners in 1870. With the help of such maps, the researcher can easily locate the property of an ancestor. In Section 26, just above Crawfordsville, the site of the 1782 burning of Colonel Crawford is marked.

more than fourteen of the presently existing Kentucky counties. Moreover, many early settlers of land which is now in Kentucky and Tennessee considered themselves to be and, in fact were, Virginians and North Carolinians, respectively. Portions of Westmoreland County, Pennsylvania, and all of what now is West Virginia were in Virginia at one time.

So, how do you solve the problem of knowing in what county records to look? It is very easy if you simply remember that unless the old county passed out of existence (became *extinct*) almost never were county records relating to land moved to a newly created county. That is, all new counties started from "scratch" with their own records. Thus, in whatever county you now find records of an ancestor, you will know that since its records commenced only at the date of its formation from other counties, you must look to the records of the earlier counties from which it was formed to continue backward through time.

Where do you look to learn the names of the old *predecessor counties*? In virtually all *county histories* (further of which later in this section), an early chapter will reveal what previous counties were carved up in order to bring that one into existence. In addition to that source, every state library has other and similar reading materials concerning the beginnings (the *genesis*) of its counties. Finally, numerous maps have been published showing boundary line changes which have taken place, such maps often keyed to the *Decennial Censuses*, which enumerations we will discuss shortly.

So, if you are to move backward in time you must learn of and do research within every one of the older counties which once had the power to tax and to govern the land occupied by a known ancestor. To not consider the genesis questions is to fail to do adequate research.

Books

Back to our discussion of the library. There, and of the greatest importance, you may expect to find the many works of previous historians and genealogists who have written family histories, histories of an area or county or state, and myriad other research aids. Those writers have *abstracted*, *extracted* from, compiled and summarized courts' records, ships passengers and servants lists, church records, marriage bonds and ceremonies, lists of veterans, tax records of all kinds, land, deed, and mortgage records, wills and estates records, obituaries and cemetery lists, lists of noblemen such as earls and knights, and many, many other sources. Most of such works are well indexed, and you must thoroughly search those indexes for books and materials covering the time periods in which an ancestor is known to have lived.

How do you use a book? Never start with the index. Commence reading, instead, with the table of contents found in the front of the book. There you will learn how the book is organized and how the author thinks the subject matter should be broken down. Then read the Preface and Introduction. Within those sections you perhaps will learn which sources were included and, most importantly, which were not included, thus saving you many hours of searching through the indexes of books which contain no information that you need. If you have not done so, go now to the Table of Contents of this book and observe how this writer thinks the subject should be divided.

Citing Sources

Having found yourself amidst materials which are important to your search, it is absolutely necessary that you make a note of the *source* from which every bit of that information comes. It is not good enough that you believe (or, indeed, are most positive) that a fact is true. If you expect researchers and family members of the future to rely upon your findings and use the same as avenues to further research, you must set forth the source from which your information came; you must provide a *reference* for your reader. Especially will that be true later when you write of that ancestor or family line. You must cite the source, and even if the source is your own experience or is a tale told to you by a grandmother, that source should be spelled out. So, when you write down a new fact, also write down the source for that fact; not later, right then.

If your source is a written record, one of several proper ways to cite it is, first, to write down the name of the author and then the book title. Next, set forth the publisher and the year of that edition, and, finally, list the page or pages upon which you found the information used. For example:

Richard L. Morton, *Colonial Virginia*, 2 volumes. University of North Carolina Press, Durham, 1960, Vol. 1, pp. 215 - 220.

It is not ever sufficient to cite, for example, "N. Car. Veterans records" or "Records of the D.A.R." You must be precise. You must provide your reader with enough information so that he or she may go seek out the same book and pages which you read and from which you quoted.

Searching For An Ancestor

You should choose but one or two names to research per trip to the library. Only when that library has been exhausted as to those names should you move to additional ancestors. Always resist the temptation to undertake the research of numerous names at the same time. Of course, if you are many miles from home you may need to search for a number of family names. Nevertheless, you still should start with but one and completely work it out before moving to others.

Just how do you undertake research of a certain ancestor or ancestral line? You need to know a name and an approximate time period. If you also know a place, you are that much ahead. Suppose you know that your grandmother was named Grace McCart before she married your grandfather John Sherill. Also suppose you know that she died about 1950, when she was about eighty years old, and that before she was married she lived somewhere in or near Smith County, Illinois, the state in which you are now researching.

Censuses

The censuses will be very important to you and are a good place to begin. There has been a U.S. Decennial Census every ten years since 1790, and therein may be found some record of most (notice that we said "most" and not "all") of those who were alive here when those censuses were taken. You will discover notable differences in the manner in which censuses were indexed in and after 1870, and much variation in the information to be gained from the different censuses. Generally speaking, the more recent the census the more information you will find there. As examples, the censuses taken in 1850 and thereafter listed the names and ages of all persons living within the household, usually their occupations, and some facts as to property they then owned, including any slaves. The slaves were not named.

However, the Census for 1840 and the *enumerations* before then name only the *Heads Of Households* (the men usually, or women if they were considered the dominant person of that residence), give only the numbers of other persons of both sexes within various age groups who were residing at that dwelling, usually provide information as to the number of slaves and servants, and but little else. So notice, for example, that if in 1840 (or at the taking of any other Decennial Census before that year) your ancestral great grandmother lived with her daughter and son-in-law, she will be shown only as a female within a certain age group and will not be listed by name in any index to that census. That daughter and son-in-law will be found indexed under his *surname* (last name) and his *given name* (first name), which, of course, was different from that of the grandmother. The same also is true of their children; since they were not named, they are not indexed.

Other helpful Census facts to remember are:
● The 1840 Census listed U.S. Pensioners, thus providing clues to prior military or governmental service by a family member;
● except for a very few counties, the 1890 Census was destroyed by fire, as were large parts of the Census of 1790;
● the censuses of and after 1880 reveal the county and state of birth of the parents of the people listed;
● the Censuses of 1900 and 1910 give the date of arrival of any immigrants there listed;
● and the 1920 Census is the most recent one available since Censuses are not open to the public until seventy-two years after their taking (the 1930 Census will be opened to the public in the year 2002).

Upon your first encounter with each of the many censuses, whether state or Federal, note carefully what information is to be found in the entries in that enumeration, and, as always, make a complete record of all of the family facts learned from those entries. Remember, when working with the Decennial Censuses be sure to use your printed forms. They are available for each national census since 1790 and are very helpful in record keeping and in citations of your sources. (The forms concerning the Decennial censuses included in this book in Appendix 1, should be kept as "masters" and copied for future use.) As said, many libraries and bookstores also sell quite inexpensive census forms.

Genealogists and others have compiled and published indexes to the censuses taken before the number of people became so great as to make the publication of the complete censuses unwieldy and prohibitively expensive. Nevertheless, even where the numbers were great, many local societies have published indexes or the censuses themselves for their county or city. So it is that you usually will find both indexes and complete censuses by states for many of the enumerations through 1840, but after that the printed volumes may be indexed only, thus requiring you to view the microfilm if you want the total information available (and you do).

Indexes quite usually are titled, for example, "Index To The 1810 Census of Virginia," and most libraries have printed censuses and indexes in the same section of the shelves. If you do not find them, ask the librarian for assistance.

When you find the name of an ancestor in the index to a census which has not been printed, you will need to go to the microfilm copy of the actual (original) census record to see the rest of the information. How do you do that? *The Index To The 1810 Census of Virginia*, for instance, relates simply that a man named "Keeler, William" is to be found at "016 Rcm." That notation means that a copy of the original entry concerning William Keeler and his family is on page 16 (016) of the Census records of Rockingham County (Rcm) for that year. The library will have an alphabetized listing of the Virginia counties for that census, along with the microfilm Roll numbers upon which those records will be found. Simply check out that microfilm roll (Rockingham 1810 happens to be Roll #67) and, using the equipment - the *viewer* - available there at the library, move forward through it to page #16. There you will find both Keeler and the numbers of the others who then were within his household.

Be aware that since the original enumerations were done the Censuses for many areas have been renumbered, sometimes several times, and the publishers of the index have utilized that enumeration which they believe to be the most recent. So, if your ancestor seems not to appear on the page listed in the Index, carefully examine that page and the ones just preceding and just ahead for other and different sequences of page numbers. Through inadvertence, you may have moved forward through the reel in a sequence which was rendered obsolete by a later page numbering yet still is visible on the film. While census indexes are quite reliable in this regard, do be careful of page numbering (*pagination*).

Once you have found your ancestor in the microfilm record, it is very important to note whether or not the names found just before and just after that ancestor are in alphabetical order. Why? If not, they likely will then be in the same order as the enumerator (census taker) found them when he traveled the roads making the count. When the names are set forth as they were encountered, the neighbors on both sides are thus revealed. As with cemeteries, always make good notes as to those neighbors. Again, why? Because quite frequently (much more so in the early days than now) neighbors were relatives or in-laws and, furthermore, families from the same neighborhood or from a local church congregation often migrated west or south together, there again to live as neighbors. The Scots and Welsh were particularly known for living and moving in groups.

Interpreting Census Records

Back to our imaginary grandmother Grace McCart Sherill. Because we know that she died about 1950 and was near eighty years old, we thereby know that Grace was born about 1870 (1950 minus 80 equals 1870), and since her maiden name was McCart, we might start with the 1880 U.S. Census for Illinois. Remember too that in addition to the Decennial Censuses, there often were state censuses which are just as important for your purposes. Ask the librarian about the existence of such other enumerations; he or she will have a list of state censuses available or will direct you to the proper catalog heading.

The indexes for the Census of 1880 and thereafter are on computer, on a system called *Soundex*. With Soundex you need only type in the last name of your ancestor and the computer will tell you on which microfilm roll you can find him or her. A significant advantage of Soundex is that you do not need to know how an ancestor's name was spelled to still be able to find them. Say, for example, that you cannot find McCart in the index because the enumerator misspelled it, or the name was originally spelled differently, or for whatever reason. You can then use Soundex to compile for you a list of all the names in the census that *sound* like McCart, such as McCurt, MacCardy, McCurdy etc., together with the microfilm roll and page number on which each appears. You can then look up each name until you find Grace and her family. The entry will give the names and details concerning the people found at that residence by the original enumerator. Soundex is easy to use, however rather than undertake here to memorize the method from this book, simply ask the librarian for assistance. Virtually all libraries have the Soundex code system set forth in an easy hand-out available for your use at the information desk.

In the 1880 Soundex you will find grandmother Grace as "McCart, Grace" (her maiden name). Suppose the 1880 entry shows Grace and her parents to have then resided in River Township of Smith County at residence "054." Check out the microfilm for that county for the year 1880, and at the beginning of that roll you will find the page number at which the entries for River township commence. Move through the film to that page, and then move still further down the page to residence #54 where the details concerning the entire household with whom she then resided will be set forth.

Suppose that there at residence 54 you find Grace to be a little girl of nine years of age. You now know that she probably was born in 1871 or thereabouts. As now, people approximated ages, hence an age given in the census as "35" might in fact really be anywhere from thirty four years and some months to very near thirty-six, depending upon the date the enumerator arrived at the house. That date is usually written at the top of each or every other page. Further, as with the other information, the ages may have been given by someone other than a parent, hence additional errors may be present.

If Grace was living with her family, that 1880 census entry also should tell you 1.) the names of her parents or guardians, 2.) their ages and occupations, 3.) their birth-places and, as mentioned, those of their parents (Grace's grandparents), 4.) whether or not the adults there named were literate, 5.) the relationship of each person living there to the Head of the Household, and 6.) the stated dollar value of both the real estate and the personal property owned by each person living within that household.

If they lived with Grace and her parents, her brothers and sisters (*siblings*) also will be listed. The eldest sibling quite usually will be listed first and the youngest last, with their birthplaces (*nativity*) and occupations set forth opposite their names. Note that if you find that the birthplace shown for one of the older children was different from that of a younger one, you have an excellent clue that during the period of time between the birth of those two children the family moved from the earlier birthplace to the later one. That information usually is an excellent clue that later will lead you to a prior state, territory, or place of residence of the family.

Moving Backwards In Time

Note that by simply subtracting the age of the eldest child shown from the year of that census, you will have an approximate year before which the marriage of the parents likely took place. So, if Grace's eldest brother was shown by the census of 1880 to have been seventeen years old, by subtracting 17 from 1880 we arrive at the year 1863 as the year of his birth, hence the year during or before which we should expect to find the marriage of his parents. In that regard, note that they may never have married; many did not. Nevertheless, by your subtraction you still will have ascertained an approximate year during which they began their lives together. Note also that the records of many marriages were not preserved, hence will never be found.

Speaking further of siblings - brothers and sisters: make careful notes of their names, especially if you have encountered those same names elsewhere in the family. Just as today, recurrent names were common, and very few families failed to name at least one child after a parent, ancestor, aunt, or uncle. While you now may not be particularly interested in such collateral lines (families of brothers and sisters and their in-laws and spouses and descendants of cousins), should you later choose to write of the family you will quite likely want to include and index their names. Further, it is probable that among the descendants of those siblings, you will find other persons researching your family. Few indeed are the families within which there has not been considerable previous research.

As noted, in years past just as now, many children were named after their parents, grandparents, or others in the family who were well liked or highly regarded, hence a recurring name within a family line may reveal to you an ancestor from whom that name first came. Perhaps no better illustration may be found than in the case of Richard Parker who lived in Virginia in the mid 1600s (the *seventeenth century*). Since the first one, there has been a Richard Parker in that family for at least nine generations. So too, the families of the Patriots George Mason and Terry Connor and the Saltonstalls of New England.

Suppose the 1880 census microfilm reveals opposite his name that the birthplace of Grace's father was Edgecombe County, North Carolina and that of her mother was Bourbon County, Kentucky. You now have a running start on that branch of the family, and after completing your Smith County work, you may continue your search for her mother in the Bourbon County and Kentucky materials, and for her father in those for Edgecombe County and Eastern North Carolina.

In that 1880 census you will also learn the ages of her parents. By simply subtracting those ages from 1880, you have their approximate birth years. Be most cautious however, for the names, numbers, and dates found in censuses are only as reliable as the enumerators and the persons who provided the information to those enumerators. Through those differing birthplaces of the father and mother, you also may have a clue concerning the location of their marriage records. As did many, when yet a young man the father may have gone from North Carolina to Kentucky, there met and married Grace's mother, after which they went to Illinois country together. Notice that since most early migration was from east to west and south, not vice versa, it would be most unlikely (yet not impossible) that the marriage took place back in North Carolina.

So check the records for Smith County, and if you do not find the marriage of Grace's parents there you then should move to the Kentucky marriages, all the while remembering that the parents may never have married or the record of that union may now be lost. If the library being searched has no further materials concerning marriages or other records of either Kentucky or North Carolina, put your notes aside as to those members of the family. You can take them up later in other libraries having more materials as to those states.

After finishing the 1880 Census search, move backwards in time; check the Census for 1870. Notice that if neither Grace nor her family appear in the 1870 Census for Smith County, then they probably moved from Kentucky or wherever to Illinois during the years 1870 - 1880. As mentioned, the approximate year and place from which that move took place may be revealed by the birthplaces of the children listed, e.g., if a three year old child was said in the 1880 census to have been born in Kentucky, yet a one year old was shown to have been born in Illinois, the period between 1878 and 1880 probably was that during which the move took place. So, think!

Having established that their move probably took place in the 1870s, you may pick up the trail by checking 1870 and the earlier censuses in those other states - Kentucky and before that North Carolina - from which places you now suspect that the family came.

After you have moved backwards through the available censuses - 1860, 1850, 1840, etc. - to the point at which Grace and her family no longer appear, go back to 1880 and start moving forward through the years to 1900, 1910, etc. (remember that the 1890 Census is probably missing), again making complete notes as to all information gained.

Reliability of Census Information

Concerning the reliability of census information, as the census takers arrived at the homes of the citizens, oftentimes the man of the house was working in the fields or was

CERTIFIED COPY OF MARRIAGE CERTIFICATE.

No. *1251*   The State of Ohio, *Wyandot* County, ss.

~~this day~~ I ~~Do Hereby~~ Certify, That ~~on the~~ .... day of .... A. D. ~~19~~ ....

I, solemnized the MARRIAGE of Mr *William L. Midlam*

with Miss *Maggie B. Carner.*

Witness my hand this 9" day of

September, A. D. 1893.   *Geo. B. Wiltsie*

Court of Common Pleas, Probate Division.

The State of Ohio, *Wyandot* County, ss.

I, *Russell H. Kear* .... Judge and Ex-Officio

Clerk of the Court of Common Pleas, Probate Division, within and for said County having

the custody of the Files, Journals and Records of said Court, do hereby certify that the fore-

going is a true copy of the Certificate of Marriage of the parties therein named, as the

same appears on the records of said Court, and I further certify that I have carefully com-

pared the foregoing copy with the original record, and that the same is a full and correct

transcript thereof. *And I further certify the record shows*

the ages to be   WITNESS my signature and the seal of said Court,

21 and 18 years   this *27* day of *July,* 19*35*

respectively.

Russell H. Kear,
Judge and Ex-Officio Clerk.

By *Daniel Reynolds*
Deputy Clerk.

Certified Copy of a Marriage Certificate
Here is a 1935 local government (an Ohio County) certification of a
marriage which took place in 1893. Notice also that the ages of the
parties are set forth, thus providing their approximate birth years.

away from home, and if the wife also was out of the house the enumerator may have gotten the family information from a child or even from a boarder, live-in, or neighbor. Further, then as now, many people, including some census takers, were not conscientious or careful. Then too, most of our ancestors were known to take a drink on a hot day to cool down or to warm themselves on a cold day. In fact, nearly everyone drank intoxicants (more by reason of an abiding distrust of the water than from a desire to be drunk, it must be said, even though, as now, that urge often was close at hand). Some enumerators were lazy, inept, or anxious to return home. So, for the reasons given, errors regularly crept into census returns.

Illiteracy

It also is important to remember that in the early days a great many folks were illiterate, hence the enumerators themselves often were required to provide the *phonetic* (how it sounded) spelling of the names told to them. Were that not problem enough, the enumerators themselves quite often had very limited educations. So, make note of any spelling variations found, and be aware that an ancestor may be found in a census under a spelling different from both the earlier and the later enumerations. In the censuses after 1850 the literacy of those enumerated was set forth.

Other Factors Causing Errors

Quill pens (usually the prime tail feathers of geese), while the best then available, nevertheless worked sporadically at best, and sometimes not at all. Especially evident are such failings when the movement of the hand was straight to either the left or to the right. Thus, a capital (upper case) letter such as "R" may appear as a "K" and "O" might look like a "U" or even as "II". An example: In an Ohio Census, William R. Drake appears quite clearly as William K. Drake, the left to right top of the letter R having been skipped by the pen.

In addition, sometimes the ink used was of poor quality and the handwriting terrible. Examples of incorrect and misleading census information are known to every researcher, and soon you too will have uncovered misleading data concerning one or more ancestors. So, always be aware of the likelihood of unintentional error, and intentional as well, as where a measure of shame was present over illegitimacy, criminal activity, etc., or a member of the family desired that his or her whereabouts not be known.

Boarders and Live-ins

As to boarders and other live-ins, keep in mind that in the early days many, perhaps even most, rural homes (and many urban households, as well) sheltered and maintained farm hands, servants, and others who, though not members of the immediate family, also were not slaves. Such folks were enumerated with that family. Further, families very often provided a home for aged parents - usually the mother, but sometimes both mother and father - and for *spinster* (unmarried) aunts, and disabled or handicapped relatives. Then too, and often, especially before the period 1840 - 1850, children were *fostered* out or *apprenticed* to another family, the former usually to provide a helping hand to the household having charge of the child while relieving the parent of the financial and physical burden of raising it, the latter serving to provide a child with training in a trade or calling in exchange for his or her labor.

Folks who were not the parents or children of the heads of household were listed following the names of those prime members. So, even though errors again were made, the prescribed order was, first, head of household, then his (or her) spouse, followed by their children beginning with the eldest and continuing through the youngest, next the parents of the head of household, then parents of the spouse, then other relatives, and lastly, any live-ins and boarders, again, with the eldest shown first.

By reason of the likelihood of live-ins, in the censuses prior to 1850 where only the Heads of Households were specifically named, when you find in any age group a larger number of people than would make sense in light of your other research, you have probably uncovered such boarders and non-direct family members. Make careful notes of the names or ages of all such live-ins. Even if they were not then, they later may have become relatives through marriage to a member of that family.

Origins of Surnames

The origin of the surname of any ancestor is very important to you. By realizing that Grace was born a "McCart", you have a clue as to her background, that is, her father's lineage. The name "McCart" is almost surely Scottish, hence her *paternal* (her father's side) ancestors quite probably once were Scottish or Scotch-Irish. The prefixes Mac- and Mc- meant "son of." So too, in Wales and Ireland; the ap- in Welsh names (ap-Griffith) and the O'- in Irish names (O'Neal) both meant "son of" (son of Griffith, son of Neal).

So, how will you find such places of origin? Either in the genealogical section or in the general reference section in nearly all libraries you will find books which discuss the histories and derivations of surnames. Look up each and every one of your family names therein, and then, not sometime later, for your future use, make good notes on that family unit chart concerning the nationality and meaning of the name. Having learned that the McCarts likely originated in Scotland, in later searching you likely will come to seek out and utilize materials having to do with that nation and its people.

The Spelling of Names

It is critical that you always remember that over the many centuries virtually every family name has been spelled in different ways. (If you want to reveal that you are a novice and new to this hobby, all you need to do is insist to an experienced researcher that your family spelled your surname in only one way.) So, be most cautious and do not assume that simply because your grandmother spelled her name in a certain way that anyone else before (or after) her did the same. For example, McCart probably once was McCarty or McCarthy or MacCardy or even McCurdy; Beatty may have been Batte, Baty, Beattie, or Beaty; the German surname Feldstein may now be Fieldstone; Schmidt may be Smith, Smithe, or Smythe, or a dozen other spellings; Blanco may now be White, and Moreno, now Brown. German names such as Knertzer may now be Kornetzer, Conatser, or Cornester; Koerner may now be Carner or Kerner or Korner or even Connor; Kessler may have been Kistler, Kestler, or Kiessler; and Schneider likely is now Snyder, yet may be Schneiter, Schneyder, Snider, or even Taylor (tailor), which is what Schneider means in German.

Then too, do not forget that for given names contractions and nicknames were used then, just as now, e.g., Jane may have been Jenny; Veronica (sounded like "Fronica" in German) often was Fronny or Franny or even Frances; Elizabeth became Betsy, Betty, Beth, Liz, Lizzy, or Libby; Rebecca was Beck or Becky; Tabitha commonly was Tabby; Bill, Billy, Will, or Willy served for William; Tommy or Tom for Thomas; Lafe for Lafayette; Hank or Harry may have been Henry; John was Jack many times, and on and on. So, always be alert for nicknames!

It also is important that you remember that the terms Sr. (Senior) and Jr. (Junior) may have meant only that a certain person was the older or the younger of two people with the same name living in the same neighborhood, and the two may not have been related at all. Note that unlike now those terms also occasionally were used when referring to women as well as men. The words sister and brother often were often used in the Biblical sense and did not refer to kinship, especially in letters and other correspondence. Then too, in the early days in-law was not a term of precise meaning and often was used when identifying, step-parents, adopted children or those who had a guardian. Cousin very often meant any relative more distant than parent or brother or sister, and just as now, children were taught to show respect by addressing such older cousins, other relatives, and even friends of the family as aunt or uncle. So, be very careful!

Cousins and "Greats"

Cousin type relationships are not difficult to figure out, and much ado has been made and nonsense written about what is really a very simple reckoning. If you and another relative have one or more common grandparents, you are first cousins. The children of such first cousins are your first cousins, once removed, and are not your second cousins. Likewise, your children are the first cousins, once removed of your first cousins. Your second cousins are those people who share with you one or more common great grandparents. Your third cousins are those people who share one or more common great-great grandparents. So, simply count the number of greats in the title of the most recent common ancestor and add one (1), and you have the degree of cousinhood. Thus, if your third-great grandfather is the most recent common ancestor of you and another person, then you and that person are fourth cousins. That person's children are your fourth cousins, once removed, and that person's grandchildren are your fourth cousins, twice removed.

Relationships of remote aunts and uncles are determined in the same way. Simply take the number of greats in an ancestor's name and add one (1) more great before the word "aunt" or "uncle" when speaking of the brothers and sisters of that ancestor. So, if a person was the sister of your grandmother (there are zero (0) "greats" in your grandmother's name), add one (1) great, and she is your great aunt (also sometimes called *grand* aunt). If a man was a brother of your great grandfather (there is one (1) great in the grandfather's title) add one more great for a total of two (2), and that brother is your great-great uncle. So, the sister of your fourth-great grandmother was your fifth-great aunt, and so on. Incidentally, do not bore or wear out your listeners by describing an ancestor as, for example, "my great-great-great-great-great grandmother." If it is important to the conversation, say "my fifth-great grandmother," if not, say simply "my ancestor."

Birth, Adoptive, and Foster Parents

If you or an ancestor were adopted or fostered out, there are ways of disentangling the prior records and learning something - often a great deal - about the birth-parents and their ancestors. The means and methods for conducting such searches are the subject of several good books and are beyond the scope of this work. Still though, remember that the best first approach to such research problems is geographical in nature. Gain all information possible as to WHERE the adopted or fostered child, the suspected birth-parents, and the adoptive or foster parents lived during the years immediately before and immediately after the birth date of the child. Your search will begin with interviews of officials and in the courthouses in those areas.

If you come upon such relationships during your research, make careful notes and glean every fact and bit of information possible from your interviewees and from everybody else having any knowledge whatever of the facts. In genealogical problem solving, no bit of information is too small or insignificant to be carefully noted. Surely that is even more true with adoption or foundling problems.

Titles And Forms Of Address

Finally in the matter of how our ancestors were addressed: in the early days the terms *Mr.* and *Mrs.* were titles and were used only when addressing or referring to persons who had gained (or inherited) position, wealth, and respect within their community. So, only if their contemporaries did so should you refer to an ancestor as either Mr. or Mrs. Often two persons with the same name may be distinguished one from the other by learning that one was addressed as Mr. while the other was not. Always remember the expression "Same name does not mean same person."

Incidentally, all early public offices were considered worthwhile and important and were sought after vigorously, hence when you find an ancestor who was, for example, a *Burgess, Justice of the Peace,* or *Constable,* you may be assured that he or she was held in considerable regard by his contemporaries and peers. Further, such persons very often were referred to as Mr. or Mrs., at least while in that position, even if they were not so addressed before and after occupying the office.

Prob. 656   Barrett Brothers, Publishers, Springfield, Ohio

CERTIFIED COPY OF BIRTH RECORD

The State of Ohio,_____Marion_____County.   **Probate Court**

Date of Record_____A. D. 1899

No. 52

Name in Full_____Delta Midlam

Date of Birth—Year 1 898, Month_____August_____, Day 13

Place of Birth—State_____Ohio_____, County____Marion

City, Town or Township____Marion

Sex_____Female

Color_____White

Name of Father_____Wm. L. Midlam

Mother's Maiden Name____Maggie Carner

Residence of Parents_____Marion, Marion Co., Ohio

By whom reported and address_____

The State of Ohio,_____Marion_____County.

I, the undersigned, certify that I am Judge of the Probate Court within and for said County, which is a Court of Record; that I am ex-officio Clerk of said Court and by law the custodian of the records and papers required by law to be kept in said Court; that among others a **Record of Births** was heretofore required by law to be kept therein; and that said person's birth has been registered according to law. Record of Births, Vol.____3____Page____143____now in this office.

WITNESS my signature and the seal of said Court, at_____Marion_____Ohio, this____10th

day of_____July_____, 19.63.

_____Edward J. Ruzzo_____
Judge and ex-officio Clerk of the Probate Court of said County

By_____Hazel Fauser_____
Deputy Clerk

Certified Copy of a Birth Record
A typical birth certification by a local government, in this case Marion County, Ohio. Note that the record dates from 1899, even though the certificate is only about thirty years old.

Researching Through The Use of Ages

As should now be more apparent even than before, when you are searching, you must think - THINK. If, as in our example, in the 1880 Census you found Grace McCart to have been nine years old, you know that she probably was born in about the year 1871 (written as circa 1871, or c. 1871, or c1871). Hence there is no point in searching for her name in records considerably before that year. Nor will she be found in any marriage records before the mid-1880s, since she was but a child during the years prior to then. Moreover, she will not be found signing documents nor paying taxes before about 1890, since she was not yet of mature years. If you learn that she had a son born in 1910, yet do not know her death date, there surely is no point in searching for her among death and estate records before the year of that birth. Remember, though, that she may appear by name at any age in church records and in all the censuses after 1840.

Notice how much time you have saved by thinking. By determining a span of years during which an event MUST have happened, you have eliminated the need to search for that event in the many records and books for those years during which that happening could not have taken place.

Speaking of ages, while quite usually anyone who was *tithable* was over sixteen, it is important to remember that in the very early years the expression *of age* did not necessarily mean that a person was eighteen or twenty-one years old. *Of age* or *of majority* often meant that the peers and the lawgivers of that day considered the person mature and able to act as an adult, regardless of the number of his or her years. Hence, while a child of six almost surely would not ever be viewed as of age, a twelve year old might. Only during the last century did the law of most states uniformly determine that twenty-one (or eighteen, sometimes) was of age. Be aware also that fourteen for a long time was (and is) an age at which children could enter into various contractual relationships and make many decisions affecting their relationships with their parents, guardians, and the world.

So, while researching, always stop and think through the problem. Pretend that you are the person being researched, such as Grace, and were born in 1871 or whenever. Then start looking in the books and materials which relate to the appropriate periods in the life of that person.

When researching someone's life in a certain state, such as Grace in Illinois, you must thoroughly search for the name in all the records for that period of time between her birth and her death or the year in which she is known to have left that county or state. Further, it is wise to check the indexes for a few years after the death or known removal of that person from the state since proceedings having to do with *estates* or inheritances from other states may not have been filed nor appear of record until sometime - often many years - later.

Time Line Drawings

While researching, simple *time line drawings* are immensely helpful to your thinking and organization of materials. On the back of that family unit chart dedicated to Grace and her husband draw a straight line for each of those marriage partners. Put their birth dates and years near the left ends of those lines and their death dates near the right ends. Divide the lines into five year periods, and each time you learn a new fact or anecdote about either of them, briefly note that information at the proper year on the time line. By so doing, a bit at a time, you will find yourself able to reconstruct a most interesting life story of Grace and her family, and the small effort involved in making such drawings also will help you remember the facts concerning that family. Always remember that genealogy is the study of lives, events, and emotions, and is not a mere gathering of names and dates.

On the backs of their family unit charts, do a similar time line sketch for each of your ancestors. Incidentally, the back of the unit chart is a fine (perhaps the best) place to write both new facts and the corresponding references concerning the members of that family unit.

Departments of Vital Statistics

After the beginning of the twentieth century (the 1900s) our states established departments to house and maintain *vital statistics* - "vita" is Latin for "life" and vital statistics are those statistics that relate to birth, deaths, marriages, health and disease. In fact, in 1914 it became Federal law that all states maintain a repository for such important records. Nevertheless, and for some years thereafter, more than a few local officials and physicians ignored or forgot to submit information concerning births, places of birth, deaths, causes of death, and names of relatives, and as a result, for a few years after 1914, the births and deaths of some ancestors did not find their way into the records of those agencies.

Those departments of government are most important to the researcher, and by addressing a letter to the Bureau of Vital Statistics at your state capitol you may procure a form which, though variously named, when filled out and returned, will provide such data as is available for the birth or the death of a particular ancestor. To utilize this source and gain *birth certificates* and *death certificates* by mail you quite usually need to know the exact date of the event (birth or death). However in most states you may visit in person, use their indexes (set forth by years or groups of years), and upon locating the ancestor order the information which will be sent to you later. The charge is usually very reasonable.

Depending upon whether you seek information concerning a birth or a death, you likely will find considerable information, often including date and place of birth, parents names, marriage dates, cause, place, and date of death, persons present, and perhaps the birthplaces and facts concerning next of kin and parents.

THE STATE OF OHIO, ::

‑   ::   SS:

COUNTY OF WYANDOT, ::

    Minnie Schwilk, being first duly sworn, says
that she is seventy-eight years of age, that she was born
in Upper Sandusky, Ohio May 16, 1857; that she has been a resident
of this county for many years.

    She further says that she is personally and well
acquainted with Maggie Carner Medlam; that the said Maggie Carner
Medlam was born in Wyandot County, Ohio in 1867; that she lived
in the house belonging to affiant's father in Mononcue, a suburb
of Upper Sandusky, Ohio when she was three years of age; that she
associated with her for many years and knows that the said Maggie
Carner Medlam is sixty-eight years of age.

    Affiant is not r e l a ted t o Maggie Carner
Medlam and has no other interest than to state the facts as she
knows them.

Minnie Schwilk

    Sworn to before me and signed in my presence
this 30th. day of July,1935.

Helen F. Fischer

      Notary Public, Wyandot County, Ohio.

Sworn Statement

*Before the keeping of vital records became widespread, it often was
necessary that one's age, condition of servitude, parentage, or past
residence be proven by the sworn statements of persons who knew of
the facts. Here a lady born in 1857 attests to the birth and prior residence of Maggie Carner who was born in 1867 in Ohio.*

So, for anyone who is known to have died after the turn of the twentieth century, you might start your search by utilizing this very valuable source. Since Grace died in 1950, if you knew the date and in what state she died you could have written for a copy of the death certificate at the same time at which you started your census work concerning her life. Funeral homes also often kept records of customers over many years, recording times of deaths, funerals, interments, who purchased the services, etc. These records are usually found in the library of the town or county in which such businesses formerly operated. They should always be checked for all family members who lived and died during the periods covered by the records.

Genealogical Clubs and Societies

Any librarian will be glad to tell you of local genealogical societies and clubs, and even if you live many miles away, you should join a society that serves an area where you have several ancestors or family lines. There are many such societies and membership is not expensive. Such organizations are made up of folks just like you, and quite usually they publish a newsletter or periodical, many of which will provide you with opportunities to run small ads (known as *queries*) seeking others who are researching family lines or ancestors that are common to you. Often a single exchange of letters will extend a family line for several generations, especially when you are new to the hobby. Many new and interesting friends will also thereby be made.

When writing to others, courtesy and custom dictate that you always include with your letter a self addressed, stamped envelope (called an *SASE*) which the recipient of your inquiry may use in responding to you. In your correspondence (and at all other times, for that matter) never hesitate to ask questions of other researchers. They too have had to solve difficult problems and usually will help. Unfortunately and occasionally you will encounter a researcher who will not help you. There are those who apparently feel that since they had to do the research, so should you. Never adopt that attitude. If we all did, research would be next to impossible.

Warning: Never think that you know so much that others can not help you, especially if you are at a "dead end" and are unable to go beyond some prior point in time. Finally, remember always that answers received from other researchers are only as reliable as they are, so always check all answers and sources for yourself.

In addition to the local societies, all states have genealogical and historical societies that are most helpful in research and in uncovering historical background and ancestry; the *Virginia Genealogical Society Journal* is but one of many. There also are regional and national organizations such as the *Tidewater Genealogical Society* and the *National Genealogical Society*; again, both of great value. Such large organizations nearly all publish very scholarly materials. If you can afford it, join one of those organizations which work in the larger perspective.

Then too, there are numerous private publishers of magazines of general interest to genealogists, but two of which are *Genealogical Helper* (Everton Publishers Inc., Logan, UT) and *Heritage Quest* (Orting, WA) (see also Appendix 3). Most libraries and many people who do family research are or have been subscribers, and usually will be happy to give you a subscription form for either. Finally in the matter of publications, you will find many dedicated to specific families, especially those with the more common surnames like Wright, Johnson, Jones, Smith, etc., or devoted to geographical areas or counties, e.g., The Rowan County Register (Ms. Jo White Linn, Salisbury, NC). Someday, you may even want to start your own such letter or journal.

In certain cases you might even want to consider calling in the assistance of a professional researchers. Such researchers are to be found in every area, often advertise in periodicals such as those mentioned above, and will be glad to assist you for usually reasonable hourly rates. Nearly always, however, your own research will be more rewarding and maybe less expensive. Caution: many who advertise their services are not as capable of searching the records as you now are, so never fail to ask for and contact references before hiring professionals. True professionals are proud of their expertise and accomplishments and will be happy to supply credentials.

Local Materials

In addition to the standard works, every library has some materials that are unique to that area and, thus, of much importance to you. Most librarians are proud of their collections and happy to discuss their materials with you. So ask them to tell you about their local records. Then, just as with your interviews, you listen and let them talk.

There is a vast quantity of local material. For example, after the invention of the typesetting machine and during the last thirty years of the nineteenth century (1800s), it became fashionable (just as now) for counties and some cities to publish histories concerning themselves and their people. Such local histories contained maps (particularly valuable) and drawings of homes (usually highly stylized, however numbers and the nature of buildings located on the properties often may be determined), anecdotes, biographies, and many other interesting facts. But, caution: Remember that the dates and details to be found in the biographical and genealogical portions of such publications quite usually were the products of the memories of those then living who usually were not genealogists, and thus errors very often were made. So, as with all materials and facts from derivative sources, be very careful and skeptical, and always confirm the information learned through other perhaps more reliable source materials.

As suggested earlier, you may check these local histories to learn from which other counties that county was carved; to learn of its genesis. If you find that in 1871 Smith County was formed from part of Madison County, then, as we have learned, Grace's parents may appear before 1871 in the records of Madison county without ever having moved.

Take the time to check local newspapers published during the three or four week period following a significant event in the life (or death) of an ancestor. Even though the original newspapers may yet exist and be found in the archives of the newspaper, the county, or the state, more often than not they are on microfilm and available in many libraries in the area. There you may find an *obituary*, a short life description, or an

Map Showing Buildings

Although stylized for placement in a county history, the researcher may approximate the number, lay-out and relative size of the buildings on these Upper Sandusky, Ohio, town lots. The map was done in 1891.

article concerning a marriage which reveals important and interesting facts previously totally unknown to you. Always gain copies of such discoveries. Keep in mind, as is true of published county histories, as a general rule newspapers were (and are) not historically terribly reliable. Those publishers were trying to market newspapers at a profit, not recording history. So exercise caution, and, as always, check your findings against more reliable sources.

In nearly all libraries you will find a group of files indexed by family name. Therein will be found clippings, letters to the library from others searching the same surnames, and written materials given to or collected by the library, most of which pertain to local families. Ask the librarian if there are such *family name files*, and if so, never fail to examine them. Such files will be in alphabetical order by surname. Be sure to submit copies of your own materials and findings for inclusion therein, in order that those who come after you also may have an easier task. Again, the materials found in such family name files are only as reliable as were the writers, and often are not carefully done. So, be skeptical and check the sources cited.

Genealogical Periodicals

Speaking of matters indexed by surnames, not to be ignored are the myriad articles concerning early families and their activities which have been written and published in the many *periodicals* (the magazines of history and genealogy) to which reference has already been made. Such fine publications as *The New York Genealogical and Biographical Record*, *The Virginia Genealogist*, *The William and Mary Quarterly*, and *The Vermont Historical Society Journal* have annual and also cumulative indexes, and over the past one hundred fifty years have identified or discussed tens of thousands of our ancestors.

Simply locate those periodicals on the library shelves, and if they are not apparent to you ask the librarian where the indexes to such publications may be found. These sources are most valuable! Never decide that your family was not important enough to have been mentioned in magazines and journals; chances are you will find several ancestors there.

Soon, thanks to the efforts of many, and to your own work as well, you will find yourself searching in colonial America. "Colonial" refers to the period and events prior to the end of the American Revolution (1783), during which we were colonies of England, France, Spain, Holland, etc.

Things were different then; we were English men and women, had kings and queens instead of Presidents; had Royal Governors instead of elected ones; permitted only male landowners to vote; approved of slave ownership in nearly all colonies (but only a few folks owned or needed any); used mostly Pounds (£), shillings (s) and pence (p), but also used French, Spanish, Dutch, and Indian money (wampum) as well as tobacco and other commodities as currency; knew virtually nothing of medicine and so died of the most common ailments (smallpox, yellow fever, malaria, pleurisy, flu, any puncture wound of the chest or abdomen, virtually all gunshot wounds, etc.); ate extremely well if wealthy and quite poorly if not so; had those who were well off and those who were poor, and almost no middle class; hunted for much of their meat and fish, and raised or bartered for the rest; heated and cooked with wood over an open fireplace; considered a husband and wife as one person, and that person was the man; believed in spirits, ghosts, apparitions, and that some people arose from the dead; either disliked or distrusted Indians; jailed people who could not pay their debts; and punished criminals with a severity now beyond our conception. Such differences are incredibly interesting, will be encountered as you research, should be included in the story of your family, and if you find an interest in such matters, many good books are available. Simply check the catalog at the library under the heading "American colonies" and "colonial life."

Indentured Servants, Redemptioners, And Criminals

Many - in fact, over 200,000 - of our colonial ancestors were *indentured servants*. Another 40,000 came here as *redemptioners* - for our purposes, nearly the same. Still another 50,000 were criminals. The servants and redemptioners were those who voluntarily exchanged labor and effort over some specific number of years of their lives (usually five to seven years or, in the case of children, generally until the age of twenty-five) for passage across the ocean to here. The criminals were guilty of everything from the most petty crimes to rape and murder and, when not so ordered, often were permitted to choose between being sent to these colonies (viewed by many as surely punishment enough for most crimes), or being sentenced to hang or spend agonizing years in an English prison. Be they servants or criminals, do not be ashamed of or embarrassed by such folks. They did something right; after all, you are the result.

There are many lists and reference works dealing with those named groups of immigrants, all of which lists must be checked, since today those servants and criminals have millions of descendants. Caution: Most of those disadvantaged early people did not here accumulate real estate nor wealth during their lifetimes, so do not presume that an early ancestor was not in a certain place simply because his or her name does not appear in the land and existing tax records for that area.

Also, keep in mind that if the children of an early ancestor were known to have lived in a certain place, the chances are good that the parents previously also were there. For the most part, the vast migrations west of the Apalachians did not get underway until the post-Revolutionary period, 180 years after the first settlement at Jamestown in Virginia.

Passenger Lists

Before you know it, through your efforts and the assistance and past work of others, you will have traced at least one line of your family to that point at which they no longer may be found in the American records. When that happens remember that all who came here came by ship; there was no other way.

You will find published many lists of ships passengers - servants and the other categories, as well - who came to this or that province or colony. Within those lists often

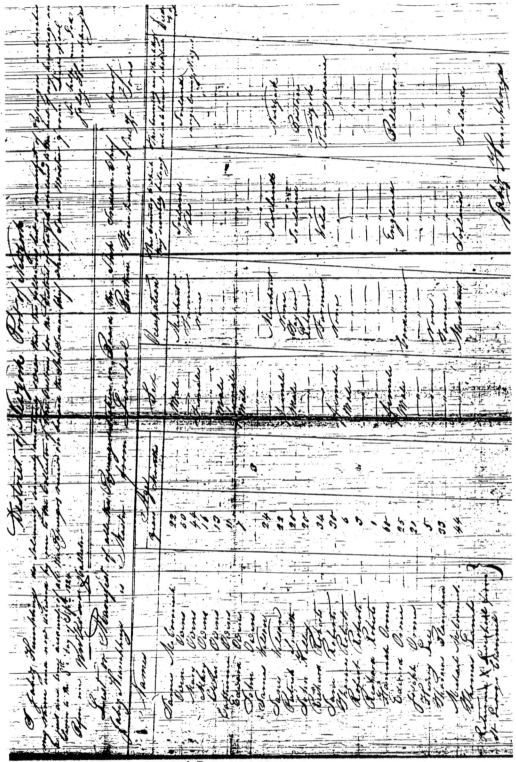

A Passenger List

This is a record of the immigration of folks from Ireland, Wales, Scotland, and England. They came to the port of New York in 1824 on the ship Indian Chief. *The record was procured from the National Archives through the use of an NATF-81 form.*

will be found the country of origin, and thereby you will find yourself contemplating a search in the "old countries." While that extended effort is outside the scope of this work, as you encounter ancestors' names in the records of those journeys and lists of travelers, remember to make careful notes for use later. Remember also that knowing WHEN an ancestor arrived here, or WHEN you lost track of him or her, will later be very important in picking up the trail in that foreign country of origin.

Keep in mind too that the passenger lists found in our libraries are far from complete. In fact, the present lists contain but three million or so immigrants, yet more than twenty one million came. Since all except the American Indians came by ship, if you do not find an ancestor in the now available lists it probably is because the record is lost or has not yet been abstracted. So, later and over the years you will want to check new passenger lists whenever and wherever such become available.

Looking Abroad

When you reach that point in the past at which a family line may no longer be found in our records, you will fully know the value of your early notes as to the origins of surnames, and you will want to research in those countries. It is likely that you will find English, German, Irish, Scotch, Dutch, Italian, and French names in your ancestry. Remember though that virtually every other nationality is somewhere represented in this great and proud nation.

Due to the ever changing conditions in their native countries, many nationalities came here during rather specific periods. For example, "McCart" is Scottish, hence, knowing that fact, at some point in time you must look toward Scotland to pick up the trail. Indeed, a Scottish or an Irish surname may reveal to you that line of your family which was a part of the Scotch-Irish immigration of the eighteenth century (1700s). During that period many Scottish folks - their ancestors having emigrated first to Ireland, especially to the area of Ulster - will be found moving to the Americas. It also may be important to your search to remember that even after that long voyage with its attendant hardships the Scotch-Irish were noted for their continuing inclinations to pick up their belongings and move to some new territory.

Then too, your Irish ancestors may have come over in the middle of the last century, during and just after the Potato Famine, a period of very difficult times in Ireland. Finally, many tens of thousands of Germans came, commencing in 1709. In fact, after the English, the Germans were the most numerous of our immigrant ancestors. So always make good notes about and use surnames as the valuable clues they are.

Using Library Catalogs

The catalog section of the library has been often mentioned. What is it and how is it used? Simply stated, a catalog is a quite complete index to the titles, authors, and subject matter to be found in that library. To use a catalog, first, look up your surnames, in case there is a written history for any of your family lines (such as the

McCarts in our example). Then too, surnames often have been extracted from books in that collection and placed in alphabetical order in a specific or separate section of the catalog, just as were the family histories written over the years.

Look in the catalog under the county name ("Smith County" in the case of your imaginary grandmother Grace) to see if there are histories of the county which you have not examined. The library may have a map collection. If so, these usually are very helpful, so look under "Maps, Smith County" and examine those. Be sure to check for titles or works under "River Township" in which Grace's family was shown by the census to have lived. Check under "veterans" for materials concerning local family members and societies. Local libraries usually will have in their catalogs lists of area marriages, burials in local cemeteries, summaries of tax records, lists of former officials and office holders, church records, and many other local materials, much of which will be found on the family history shelves, with the balance in the *stacks*. By that time, you will have a feel for the locale, and you should be able to continue in the catalog search.

Books in the stacks must be specifically requested of the librarian, usually through the use of a *call slip* filled in with the *call numbers* you found in the catalog. The call numbers are quite usually in the upper left hand corner of the card found in the catalog. As always, ask the librarian for help if you need it.

In virtually every library, in addition to the books, newspapers, and censuses mentioned, there are many additional records preserved on *microfilm* or *microfiche*. Microfilm and microfiche are photographic copies of source materials, and are indexed and cataloged in the same manner as if they were printed. Quite usually, the library will have a list showing the categories of such materials available, and will have easy to use film readers, which are the machines used for viewing microfilm and microfiche.

In addition to those films and books owned by the local facility, thousands of others are available through rental services and *inter-library loan*. For a modest fee, the librarian will procure such other records for you to examine at your leisure. This feature is most important, since it opens up to you the collections of many of the great libraries of the world. Through its use, even in a small library you will be able to do extensive family research.

Note also that any branch of the Church of Jesus Christ of Latter Day Saints (the Mormons, previously mentioned) either will have research facilities for or will provide information as to another nearby Mormon church that does have such materials available. Such *Family History Centers*, as they are called, provide access to the vast resources of their organization and the library in Salt Lake City. You need but make contact with the local church through the phone directory, and there inquire after the facilities, hours, and services available in your area.

The Mormons are most helpful, and their resources are incredibly vast. Remember however, that even though they have tens of thousands of original documents and thousands of books, as with all libraries, a large part of their collection is made up of the writings of those who are untrained, and so, as with all derivative sources, are only as good as were the authors of those writings. Still though, their library is the largest of all in this country and probably in the world, and you should make full use of this source.

By this time, it should be apparent that good library research commences long before you leave home. And well it should; after all, if you are willing to spend the time, effort, and money to make the trip to a library, even if the distance is but a couple of miles, surely it is worth an hour or so of organizational effort prior to leaving the house.

As mentioned earlier, you will not be able to accomplish all of your objectives in one visit. So, select the names of two or three ancestors whose records you are likely to find in the library to be visited. Make a determination as to what categories of records you there intend to exhaust (marriage, death, birth, military service, church records, newspapers, county histories, property maps, estate records, deed and court abstracts, etc.). Then determine those years within which you must search for specific records for those persons. For example, for the years during which an ancestor was between fifteen and twenty-five years old, you will seek a marriage record; for the fifteen to thirty year period prior to a marriage you will seek the birth record; and you will search for the records of those wars fought during the years when an ancestor was of the age group likely to have been involved (between fifteen and fifty for wars up to and including the Civil War, and between about eighteen and forty or so for the wars since then).

You will become sophisticated at the process of planning library visits sooner than you now suspect. Remember the simple rule: 1) Write down the ancestors' names to be researched; 2) determine the type or categories of records to be searched for each; and 3) establish the span of years over which you will search within those particular records. Thus, "Names, Records, and Years" before you leave home, and then, until you have finished that effort, resist the temptation to wander to other records or family lines.

Migration Routes

The movements of settlers have been previously mentioned, and it is important that you be aware of some of the routes and reasons by and for which your ancestors ended up in certain places. Generally speaking, the routes used in the long journey west followed age-old Indian trails and animal paths, which in turn were dictated by land barriers and waterways. Migrations and the westward movement are as much a part of the American personality as is our language, and knowledge of the roads, terrain, and rivers is vital to an understanding of that most interesting part of our heritage.

The reasons (and there were many) for which people went south and west often provide valuable clues in the search for ancestors. As the population grew in any area the price of land increased and the availability decreased. After but a few decades of farming the soil was depleted, jobs became scarce, and restlessness overtook some. The population increased with the birth of children and the arrival of new immigrants who also sought work and new land, and whose presence served to compound the problems. Families grew up, and the younger members had no land to farm even if they were so inclined. Some fled the law and their own past and, incidentally, sometimes took new names, thereby creating "dead ends" for their descendant/researchers of today. Some, such as the Scotch-Irish already mentioned, came with a history of wanderlust; "itchy feet", as it was called.

For those and many other reasons, great pressure was exerted upon Eastern folks who were not firmly settled to move northwest, west, and south into the more sparsely settled frontier territories. As an example of how such migration patterns may be helpful, consider that in the eighteenth century (1700s), the Pennsylvania Dutch especially ("Dutch" as in "Deutsch", not as in Holland; the Germans), and others as well, moved from eastern Pennsylvania down the Great Philadelphia Wagon Road (now parallel to I-81) through the Shenandoah Valley to the central and western Carolinas, there to join the Virginians and others who also were moving south and west.

The next generation or so then moved west through Cumberland Gap and across Wilderness Road, thence northwest to Kentucky, Ohio, Indiana, and Illinois, or southwest across Walton Road to Nashville, Memphis, and beyond. At about the same period, many Easterners (again, the "Dutch" and others), either overland or up the St. Lawrence River and then through the Great Lakes, made the long journey to the western counties of New York and Pennsylvania or to northern Ohio, Wisconsin, and Michigan. Many of these New Englanders also went to Pittsburgh, and from there down the Ohio River to that same country to which their long-missing Yankee cousins had gone via the Carolinas and Kentucky.

Nearly all libraries can and will direct you to reading materials concerning the many routes used in such westward movements. If someday you are at a dead end and all else has failed, as a result of the dominant migration patterns you very well may be able to pick up the trail by searching to the east and northeast from the last known location of the ancestor.

Summary

So, our libraries are the place to look for family histories, censuses, abstracts, extracts, compilations, microfilm, newspapers, and the myriad genealogical writings of others. However for most of the original records of any county or area, you must visit the courthouses.

4

Courthouses

As are the archives of the states and our nation, courthouses are collections of archival materials, and unlike libraries, which contain mostly *abstracts, extracts, summaries,* and comments derived from and concerning original records, the courthouses and the other governmental offices are *repositories* of the original or near original records and writings of times past. Such documents and mementos make up a large portion of the total materials from which we trace our roots and upon which our governments at all levels are founded. Further, although we usually do not think of them as archives, national parks, shrines, historical sites, battlefields, and departments of government quite often have some of the documentary and historical materials and mementos that have to do with the origins of their peculiar aspect of government or history.

Just as the American collections in substantial part are housed in the places mentioned and the counties' records are in the local courthouses and offices, the collection of original letters, documents, photos, and the family Bible to be found among your own belongings comprise your family archives and are equally valuable sources of historical materials, at least to you and your family. Since most of the records found in family collections have not yet been the subjects of publication by genealogists, no references to these materials usually will be found in the libraries.

In addition to being of patriotic and historical value, because such archival collections of records and artifacts remain almost unchanged since originally written or produced and thus represent the closest approach we have to the thoughts and ideas there set forth, they serve as the most reliable of the materials with which we can do research. We can come no closer to the truth of what occurred than through use of such original and near original records. (We say "near original" since a large portion of the early records are copies of still earlier ones which are now gone, especially in courthouses.)

While many of the early documents and source materials are carefully preserved, often guarded, and may be used only with great care, most are available to you for examination and study. As noted in the section concerned with libraries, those that are not open to general use often have been copied photographically - photos, microfilm, and microfiche. When such old records are open to the public, the keepers and custodians of these materials usually have rules concerning the use of the same, which rules will be explained to you upon your first visit there. You must abide by them.

In large part the records found in our courthouses contain the original source materials having to do with the local government and its citizenry. Land, tax, death, and court records concerning the rich and the poor alike were kept so that law and order could be maintained, taxes collected, and that title to property might pass from one person or generation to another with a minimum of difficulty. Unless a courthouse was burned or the records otherwise destroyed (and many were), most of those materials still exist for your pleasure and use. As examples, just as the Union armies destroyed Columbia and Richmond during the last days of the Civil War, the British burned Washington during the War of 1812. In both cases countless records of the Confederacy, South Carolina, Virginia, and the Federal government were thereby destroyed and lost forever (including, incidentally, large portions of the Census of 1790 for Virginia).

So, while libraries for the most part (but not always) have only materials derived from earlier sources (often called derivative sources) that save you both work and travel, you will want to view and gain copies of the original and complete documents, deeds, wills, artifacts, and those other records to which you have found references, as well as those that have not yet been abstracted. Therefore, you must search in the archives and courthouses of all those jurisdictions where members of your family once lived.

Courthouse documents can be great fun. We know of one researcher who learned at a Virginia courthouse that one of his ancestors who died in 1698 had eight head of cattle, including a cow named "Madam"! A Kentucky resident who died in 1804 left to his daughter a cow named "Peggy, with a bell on her." In the 1679 inventory of the assets of her seventh-great grandmother another researcher found four musical instruments: a recorder (musical instrument), two flutes, and an "hautboy" (oboe), a most unusual collection for that very early period.

Starting Courthouse Research

So then, how do you approach the task of doing research in the local archives - the courthouses? As a general rule, unlike in the libraries, you may expect to find courthouse records organized in the order in which the events happened, that is, in *chronological* order, with alphabetical indexes covering specific time periods. So, the first rule is: before entering the courthouse fix firmly in your mind their names and that time period during which specific ancestors are thought to have lived within that county or jurisdiction. (Federal courts have jurisdiction over areas which may or may not coincide with state lines.)

Stop and think back over your own life. Many records of your activities are in the courthouses where you have lived. To name but a few: your birth record; if issued locally, your driver's license; sometimes a record concerning your education or the schools you attended; your marriages; your military records and discharge; the documents showing the debts for your cars or furniture (*chattel mortgages*, financing statements, and other documentary materials required by the law when financing is done); the taxes and *assessments* levied on your properties by local government; your *real estate* purchases; any *mortgages* or *deeds of trust* on such properties; *liens* filed by or against you; lawsuits, divorces, and adoption proceedings in which you were involved; any *lunacy* records and criminal proceedings; public offices held; petit and grand jury service performed; and someday your death and estate records, to name but a few. Many, but not all, of these same records appear in some courthouse somewhere for most of your ancestors. Your task is to find which courthouses and to search the records therein.

A very large percentage of courthouse research involves property and the ownership of it. Indeed, records having to do with taxes, dispositions of the assets of dead people, and land are concerned with little else. Accordingly, you will benefit by remembering a few definitions for the words you may expect to encounter. For our purposes, your assets are everything you own of whatever nature and kind, and wherever located. Your liabilities are your total obligations to anyone, no matter of what nature those liabilities may be.

Of your assets, you doubtless own property of some sort or another. Property may be divided into two categories, a) *real property*, also called *realty* (real estate - land), and b) *personal property*, also called *personalty*, which category consists of ALL your property other than real property. Personal property may be divided into *tangibles* (automobiles, cattle, clothing, dishes, etc.) and *intangibles* (claims against others, *accounts receivable, corporate stock, bonds, promissory notes*, etc.).

So, having arrived at the county courthouse with a time period and an ancestor or two firmly in mind, how do you start? First, do not be intimidated or afraid of the surroundings. As Americans, we have been taught that our courts and courthouses are places of great solemnity, and that is as it should be. Nevertheless, most of the records of those who went before us are there for our careful use, so do not hesitate to jump in.

Maps

If you have not already gained a map of the area, here it really will be critical. Go first to the office of the *County Engineer* (he or she may be called the *County Surveyor*) or to that of the *Tax Assessor*; one or the other should be able to supply a map of the county or perhaps a *topo* such as mentioned earlier. Also and often, an historical map or a landowners map (reproductions of earlier maps of the county) will be available for minimal sums. If so, as suggested earlier, such maps are very helpful since they often show the names of early landowners, communities that no longer exist, early roads, cemeteries and churches, old forts or Indian landmarks, and other places of interest. No matter which type may be available, remember that any map is better than no map, since if you have one at hand you will be able to spot the places to which references are made in the records being searched. As a result, such locations will be much more meaningful to you.

As is true of libraries, most courthouse materials are carefully indexed. Now, while the indexes found in one courthouse will be organized in very much the same manner as those found in every other courthouse, you will encounter minor variations. Always try to figure out the indexes for yourself, and if you can not, then, and only then, ask for help from the folks in charge. Almost always, they will help you. Even more so than with librarians, courthouse personnel have no interest in your family tales; they are working, and have but little time to chat concerning ancestors.

Legal Terms

Legal documents and the words of lawyers are not difficult to read and understand, even though at first some of the words will be foreign to you. Words like *said, aforesaid, hereinafter, hereinbefore,* as well as the many Latin words and phrases formerly used all were the products of the efforts by judges and lawyers to be precise in setting forth the rights and duties of the parties involved.

Even now, many old legal terms are still in use, and many still carry the Latin endings *-or* and *-ee.* Generally speaking, the -or ending (*suffix*) designates the person bringing about or performing the action described in the document, and the -ee suffix identifies the recipient or beneficiary of that effort or action. Thus, in deeds the seller or person transferring the property to another is called the *grantor,* and the buyer - the person receiving that property - is said to be a *grantee.* Likewise with a *mortgagor* and *mortgagee;* a *lienor* and a *lienee;* a *vendor* (seller) and *vendee* (buyer), etc.

Deeds

Deeds and most other records pertaining to land are found within the courthouses in the offices of the *Register of Deeds.* The Registers' offices also may be called the offices of the *Clerk To The Court,* the offices of the *Registrar,* or by yet some other name. If none of those titles appear on the courthouse *directory* (usually found on a wall in the main hall) ask anyone working in any courthouse office where the deed records are, and they surely will point you in the right direction.

Deeds and *instruments* for the transfer or sale of land are divided into several categories, and for our purposes, five types are of importance. They are the *mortgage deeds, deeds of trust, warranty deeds, quit-claims,* and *deeds of partition.*

Now, of recent years the deed records, no matter of which of the above types, have been indexed in two ways. One set of indexes is in the names of the grantors, called the *Grantor Indexes* or *Direct Indexes,* depending on which county and state you are in. Usually located on the same shelf, or close at hand, will be found the other set of indexes keyed in the names of the Grantees. These volumes, in turn, are known as the *Grantee Indexes* or *Reverse Indexes.*

Because of the extensive borrowing of money against land, especially during this century, a great number of mortgage deeds and deeds of trust have been recorded, as a result of which those categories of deeds are now in separate volumes and have their own indexes. Remember though, such was not the case in the early days, when all deeds usually appeared in the same volumes and were indexed together.

Always remember that if an ancestor ever was a grantee (hence, as said, bought or received property), later (whether voluntarily or not) when the property was sold or transferred away he or she also had to have then been a grantor. So, when you look under "McCart" in the Grantee Index and find a deed by which Grace's family bought property, you next need to look under their name in the Grantor Index for subsequent the Murgatroyds — The twenty seventh day of January Anna Domini 1797 Before me Hilary Baker Esquire Mayor of the City of Philadelphia in the Commonwealth of Pennsylvania came the above named Amos Wickersham and acknowledged the above written Deed Poll to be his Act and Deed and desired the same may be recorded as such Witness my Hand and Seal Hilary Baker Mayor — Recorded the 8th Day of August 1800 P. Sed. Simpson Record.

**Anthony Carner
Bill of Sale to
John Kleckner**

Know all Persons whom it may concern that I Anthony Carner Blacksmith of West Buffaloe Township in the County of Northumberland and State of Pennsylvania for and in Consideration of the Sum of One hundred Pounds of lawfull money of the State of Penn. to me in hand paid by John Kleckner Tavernkeeper of the same place the receipt whereof I do hereby acknowledge have bargained sold and delivered and by these Presents according to due form of Law do bargain sell deliver and convey unto the said John Kleckner three head of Horses two Yoak of Draft Oxen two milch Cows, two heifers and one Steer two Beds and bedding, one burroe two chests and every thing therein and all the dresser furniture with two Stacks of Rye at the Widow McCalos one Stack of Rye at my own House and oats and one Stack of Rye and one Stack of Wheat at Jacob Winegarners and a set of Smith tools, five Sheep, five Hogs and all the grain in the Ground an old Still and Vessels two spinning wheels and one large wheel and all the Household furniture that I now possess, one new Waggon and Hay, to have and to hold the said bargained Premises unto the said John Kleckner his Heirs and Assigns And I the said Anthony Carner for myself my executors and Administrators the said bargained Premises unto the said Jno Kleckner his Executors Administrators and Assigns against all Persons shall and will Warrant and for ever defend, Provided nevertheless that if I the said Anthony Carner my executors Administrators and Assigns or any of us do and shall well and truly pay or cause to be paid unto the said John Kleckner his heirs or Assigns the Sum of One hundred Pounds as Principal lawful money of Pennsylvania with Interest for Redemption of the bargained Premises at any time in the space of five years from the date hereof then this Present Bill of Sale shall be void and of no effect but if default be made in the payment of the said One hundred Pounds in part or in whole contrary to the manner and form aforesaid that then it shall remain and continue in full force and Virtue In Witness whereof I have hereunto set my hand and seal this ninth day of August one thousand eight hundred — Anthony Carner Witness Present, the words new Waggon and Hay was interlined before Signing Richard N. Bashick, G Youngman, — North. County ss. Before me George Youngman Esq. one of the Justices of the Peace in and for said County Personally appeared Anthony Carner in the foregoing Instrument of writing named and did acknowledge the same his Act and Deed and desired the same may be Recorded as such according to Law. In Testimony whereof I have set my hand and seal this ninth day of August AD 1800 G. Youngman — Recorded the 11th day of August 1800. P. Sed. Simpson Al.

David Kincaid   This Indenture made the twentieth day of August in the year of our Lord one thou–

1800 Mortgage

Here is a real genealogical treasure: a Pennsylvania mortgage of personal property dated August 9, 1800, and recorded in the deed book. Note that it is called a Bill of Sale even though it is a true mortgage, and that it reveals that Anthony Carner was a blacksmith. It also shows Carners whereabouts at the time and that he owned horses, oxen, sheep, cows, a still, a "new wagon," furniture, two spinning wheels, crops, and much more. The document also prescribes the terms of payment of the mortgage.

years for the deed by which they later sold that same tract. By finding both documents, you not only will know when they moved from the property, but also may discover interesting facts previously not known to you.

Sometimes, yet fortunately not as often as some writers would suggest, deeds were not recorded, hence occasionally one of the documents (the one by which they bought the land or the one by which they sold it) will not be found, and sometimes neither one. Instances in which deeds were not executed and recorded quite usually came about, not through oversight or neglect, but through an abandonment of the property or, more often, through the death of the owner. At death, of course, there was no one to sign the deed, and it really was unnecessary anyhow, since at the moment of death the land automatically went to whoever in the eyes of the law should have it. Note that where a person was *divested* of ownership for failure to pay taxes or through some other proceeding of law, quite usually there was a deed made in the name of that person as the grantor, the same executed by a sheriff or other officer appointed by the court for that purpose.

Caution: For many of the very early records, there was but one index, and a transfer of property was often listed in that single index either by the grantor only or by both grantor and grantee. If only the grantors are listed therein, you only will find the deed by which your ancestor sold the property. However, that deed also may tell you from whom it was purchased. If so, take the name of the person who sold the land to your ancestor and search for that name in the earlier index volumes until you find the deed by which the property was deeded by that person to your ancestor.

Mortgages

Mortgage deeds transfer *title* in property from the borrower (the *mortgagor*) to the lender (the *mortgagee*). In mortgages (and deeds of trust discussed below) the land serves as security for the loan made to the mortgagor, with the condition that when the money is paid back, the lender will *release* the mortgage, i.e., cause the land rights to revert to the borrower. Since banks as we know them were uncommon (indeed, in the very early days, totally unknown), and since from the earliest times people have been willing to loan money to their kinfolks, early mortgages oftentimes set forth family relationships previously unknown.

With mortgages, unlike deeds, your ancestor probably will appear only in the original mortgage as a mortgagor, since the release back to that borrower usually was (and still is) noted only on the margin of the original recorded mortgage deed. When such releases are found, note the date, for (just as now) it may signify a move, a death, or perhaps a subsequent purchase of land by that same ancestor.

As noted, in the early days mortgages were generally recorded in the same volumes as all other deeds, so be careful and do not presume there was a sale or purchase of land by an ancestor until you read the entirety of the recorded document. If it provides (and many different expressions may have been used to do so, most located near the end of the document) that upon the payment of a sum of money, the transfer will no longer be effective or valid, then that document is a mortgage and is not a deed. So, be careful to distinguish mortgages from deeds.

Mortgages are indexed in the same fashion as are ordinary deeds - by mortgagor and mortgagee. So, simply search in the mortgagor indexes for the names of any ancestors who may have borrowed money and pledged their land as security. These fascinating documents should not be overlooked.

Deeds of trust (sometimes imprecisely called mortgage deeds of trust) are quite similar in purpose to mortgage deeds. However, in trust deeds, by reason of a past deep and abiding distrust of banks and monied people, the title to the real estate is transferred, rather than to the lender, to a third party who was approved by both the borrower and the lender and who, in turn, had an obligation to transfer the property to the lender if the debt was not paid or, instead, back to that borrower if the debt was paid as agreed. Remember that since in the early days, much more often than now, the parties and witnesses were relatives, grantees in trust deeds, if not kin, usually were well known to or lived near the borrower or the lender, or to both. Again then, clues as to residency and kinship very often may be found in the names of the trustees and witnesses in such deeds.

So, if a mortgage or the *obligation* set forth in a trust deed was not paid as agreed, just as now, the property went to the lender, thus revealing to you that hard times may have befallen your ancestors. Incidentally, hard times were common then. There was no social security, no welfare, nor were there any credit cards or food stamps. Furthermore, they jailed people for not being able to pay their bills, and whether such *debtors* were at fault or victims of circumstance was scarcely considered. So, do not find fault with your ancestors until you have learned why they suffered financial difficulties. Never make judgments nor apologies for those who went before; what was, was.

Warranty Deeds

Most transfers of land to ordinary buyers were, and still are, accomplished by the use of *warranty deeds*. As the name suggests, such deeds convey land with warranties as to the quality and quantity of the ownership being transferred. By reason of the sanctity of the ownership of land in the minds of particularly the English speaking peoples, and because of the importance to a buyer of proper title warranties and assurances that he was receiving everything for which he was paying, warranty deeds usually recite from whom the seller previously had purchased or received the property, commonly contain quite accurate descriptions of the boundaries of the land transferred, and are specific in all other details. The *spouses* (wives or husbands) of both the seller and the buyer usually were named and in the former case always required to sign. So it is that warranty deeds often reveal clues, names, relationships, and property descriptions nowhere else to be found.

One narrow ax & killing Ho —
2 buckley Bottles
2 quart Bottles
one Large Punch Bool
one Indiff Bottle
2 Small Drinks
one Tin funnel & Sass Pan
one Pewter Bason
one pint mug —
2 pr of Cards
2 lb of Spun Cotton
one Bred draft
one frying pan
2 puter plates
11 puter spoons
one puter Porringer
5 lb 3 quarters of Seed Cotton
one Small Jugg & meel Bag
one Testament & woman's Cloak
2 Duck Blankets
2 Chaff Beds —

one Ticking Bagg
2 pr of Collars and hames
one parsell of wool
one Drinking Glass
16 lb of Soap
one Brest plate
one Box Iron
one persell of old Iron
2 lb of Tallar
1 old Chear
one pr of Shews
5 Dungel Fowls
one Table
one Large Looking Glass
1 lb of pekt Cotton and Chest
one meel Sifter
one Large Baskit
one Horse
Three Cats —
Lazarus Drake

Inventory

In 1765, and as a result of a court order, a Constable seized assets of the Jones family. His list was spelled phonetically, making it possible to know how he pronounced some of the words. He quite clearly had a Virginian accent as witnessed by "Punch Bool" (bowl), "Sass Pan" (sauce), "percell of old Iron" (parcel), two pounds of "Taller" (tallow), "1 old Chear" (chair), "one pr. of Shews" (shoes, with a long e), "5 Dungel Fowls" (dung hill-chickens), "pekt cotton" (picked) and "baskit" (basket).

Marriages, Children, and Deaths

Deeds often state other interesting and genealogically important facts. They often recite prior places of residence of the parties, e.g., "John Drake of Surry county, Grantor." Since even in the earliest days, a wife was required to sign her husband's deeds and thereby dispose of her *dower interests* (*inchoate rights*), the absence of such a spousal signature almost always reveals that either the ancestor had not yet married or that the wife had previously died. So, be alert to the absence of any mention of or the signature or mark of a spouse. If no spouse signed a deed conveying land, you are safe to presume she did not exist at the time.

In the early days, perhaps more so than now, men and women needed each other to share in the never-ending, often brutalizing task of surviving. So it was that folks married, first when the men were twenty-five or so and the women at twenty or thereabouts, and upon the death of their spouses, married again two, three, or more times. Since romantic love very often was not a prime consideration, re-marriages often took place within a few months or even weeks after the death of the mate. So, do not be shocked nor make judgments if your ancestor had a new husband or wife a month after the prior one died.

The absence of contraceptives in the early days resulted in children being born every twenty four to thirty-six months commencing at marriage and continuing throughout all the childbearing years of the woman. Incidentally, the childbearing years of women usually were over by about age forty-five. Then too, many women died during childbirth or shortly afterwards from sheer exhaustion or lack of medical care (and knowledge). About one out of every five children died during infancy or early childhood.

In fact, over a period of twenty-five years a wealthy sister of the Patriot George Mason bore ten children, only five of whom grew to adulthood. Thus, in analyzing a family, if the ancestor had five children who lived to adulthood, presume that at least one died as a child, for a total of six births. Then too, if you find a list of children whose ages were two or three years apart and there is a gap or break of three or four years between two of the children, it is quite likely that either the wife died and the husband remarried during that interval, or that a child died.

Quit-claims

Back to deeds and another category of documents: *quit-claims*, often - though, again, imprecisely - called quit-claim deeds (it can be argued that a quit-claim is not a deed at all since it may convey no interest whatever and deeds always do). Unlike warranty deeds, quit-claims make no representations as to the adequacy, quality, or quantity of the sellers' title, and so have often been used by heirs to transfer their less than total interests to other heirs. As an example, suppose your father recently died *intestate* (without a will) and left as survivors your mother and four children (you and your three siblings). In most states, your mother would receive one third (1/3) of your father's property, and you four children would share equally in the remaining two thirds (2/3) of those assets.

Please take notice that I claim the benefit
of the 5th Section of the Act of Assembly, of 14th
April 1851, And elect to take Real Estate under
the same as widow of the said John Carner dec.
deceased. And I request that you cause the
whole of the following described premises to be
appraised, or such portion as may be selected
to the value of Three Hundred Dollars, to be
appraised and set apart for my use, and
that of my family, agreeably to said Act of
Assembly. viz All that certain messuage or lot
of ground, Situate, lying and being in Walker
Township Centre County Penna. Beginning at Stones
South thirty one and a half degrees East Twelve
perches along Hublers town Lots to a Post, thence
South Forty seven degrees West, along Street nine
perches to Post, thence thirty one & half degrees
West Twelve perches to Post, thence North Forty
seven Degrees East nine perches to Stones at
the Place of Beginning

Very Respectfully

Elizabeth Carner
+ mark

A.D. 1864

Request for the Division of Property after a Death
Here is a record of the 1864 election by a widow to take a portion of
real estate owned by her late husband in lieu of her right to receive
cash equal to one third the value of the total assets. Note that this leads
the researcher to the deed books for a record of the later sale of the rest
of the property by the executor.

So, you and your brothers and sisters would receive one fourth of two thirds (1/4 of 2/3), or one sixth (1/6) of the property each. Then, if all parties - mother, brothers, and sisters - agreed that you should have the land, quit-claims naming you as grantee would be *executed* (signed) by your mother and each of the other three children. Those quit-claims, then, would transfer a total of five sixths (5/6) of the property to you and serve to reunite in you all the title. Remember, you already had received one sixth when your father died. Notice that in such common cases there would be no deed from the father to anyone, since he died intestate while owning the land.

The genealogical value of quit-claims is that such instruments frequently recite the names of parents, of all of the known children, and sometimes even grandparents from whom the property or other assets might have originally come. It is very important to note, however, that occasionally, in the past and now, quit-claims have been executed by those who might have an interest, yet in fact probably do not. Accordingly, do not presume that the execution of a quit-claim in and of itself establishes ownership, ancestry, or kinship. It always is wise to cross check the information learned from quit-claims by examining the determinations made by the court in the settling of the estate (the same is discussed hereafter).

A further caution: In the early days, as now, the laws concerning intestate death (death without a will) varied widely. Hence, if you seek to determine relationship or percentage of ownership where an intestate death has occurred, the law of the time period for that particular state or colony must be checked. Not only did the law vary, but in early times, by reason of the then prevailing law and *primogeniture*, first born sons very often received all assets owned by the father, with but an allowance (dower) or rights in the income from the property going to the widow.

As an interesting example of primogeniture, it is believed that when the wealthy William Huntt died intestate in Virginia in 1668, his first son William, Jr., received the entirety of his father's assets, less an allowance to the widow, Judith, for life as her maintenance. Judith then was remarried to a wealthy widower with sons. Next, Judith had a son by the new husband, and then the husband died - once again, intestate. Then Judith died intestate. The result, unfair as it may now seem, was that, despite all the wealth, the new son got nothing from any of the deaths since both fathers had earlier sons who inherited all of their assets, and the mother Judith, being a married woman, by law owned nothing, except for her personal property which went to her eldest son.

Deeds of Partition

The last category consists of *deeds of partition*. Sometimes as a result of differences among family members in their claims against an estate, or as a result of a lawsuit by one heir or joint owner against other heirs or joint owners, a court is called upon to make a physical or financial division of property, including a partition of the real estate. In such cases, if the court finds that to make a division of the real estate it must determine the degree of kinship among the parties, then the deeds resulting from that court action - usually called deeds of partition - very often will name all of the heirs, and

In Witness Whereof

In Witness Whereof *the said Grantor*s, C. E. Carner, Alice Etherton, Hattie Fetter, James Midlam, Henry Wisher, Martin Wisher and Carl Wisher, unmarried, and Mary Carner, wife of C. E. Carner, William Etherton, husband of Alice Etherton, Jacob Fetter, husband of Hattie Fetter, Myrtle Midlam, wife of James Midlam, Hattie Wisher, wife of Henry Wisher, Maggie Wisher, wife of Martin Wisher, all of whom,

~~and~~ hereby release   their   right   of dower in the premises, ha ve

hereunto set   their   hand s ,this   6th   day of   May,

in the year of our Lord one thousand nine hundred and   nineteen.   (19 19)

Signed and acknowledged in presence of

J. M. Strelitz	Witness to signatures 1 to # 4 and 9 and 10
Mildred Stutz	
No witness required in Pennsylvania	Witness to signatures 7 and 8
Laura Orrison	Witness as to Signature 9 and 10
J. M. Strelitz	
W. A. Early	witness to 5 + 6
H. M. Fife	
N. E. Carter	witnesses to Martin Wisher Maggie Wisher
Earl B Carter	
H. C. Chambers	witness for no 13
Wheeler Went	

1 C. E. Carner
2 Mary E Carner
3 Alice Eatherton
4 William Etherton
5 Hattie Fetter
6 Jacob Fetter
7 James Midlam (seal)
8 Myrtle Midlam (seal)
9 Henry Wisher
10 Hattie Wisher
11 Martin Wisher
12 Maggie Wisher
13 Carl Wisher

Deeds of Partition and Quit-Claims

As a result of a partition suit, the persons described in the suit as "all the heirs at law of John Midlam, deceased" quit-claim their interest in land to W.L. Midlam.

also the degree of the relationship of each to the other, or to the dead person, or to both. Measures of relationships like these are called degrees of *consanguinity* if the relationship is "by blood", or degrees of *affinity* if the relationship is through marriage. Deeds of partition will be found in a) the deed records in the Register's (clerk's, etc.) office, indexed in both the grantor and grantee index volumes, b.) or in the courts' minutes (see below), or c.) in the court file (usually found in the office of the *prothonotary* (clerk of the court), or in all three places. Such Courts' files nearly always are indexed in the names of all of the parties to the lawsuit, hence are easy to seek out.

Considerations In Deeds

As to deeds in general, the money or other thing of value given or paid by the grantee to the grantor, called the *consideration*, often is very important to the researcher. When reading deeds, the consideration will be stated in the first part of the document and should be read very carefully. The traditional phrase used to describe consideration is "...in consideration of the sum of $ _(an amount will here appear)_, the receipt and sufficiency of which is hereby acknowledged...." Note too, that since in the early days and now property often was transferred to relatives in consideration of "love and affection" or in exchange for care, those or similar words sometimes will appear in the consideration clause instead of an amount of money. So again, such statements reveal family relationships and also serve to add color and detail to the stories of the lives of our ancestors.

As mentioned in the section on libraries, until the Revolution the American colonies used English money; Pounds (£), Shillings (S or s), and pence (d or p). However, after our independence many Americans found the use of anything English to be quite repugnant, and so until we had an established currency some years later many merchants and the new states (former colonies) printed, circulated, and dealt in their own money. Occasionally, too, Spanish and French currency were used (Francs, Pieces of Eight, etc.). Further, *negotiable instruments* (bills of exchange, bills of lading, warehouse receipts especially for tobacco, cotton, and grain, etc.) were circulated widely and used as money.

The result was that such "money" sometimes turned out to be worthless. In cases where the deeds revealed a type of currency that did turn out to be of no value, the sellers had the written proof needed to void the transactions. Thus, unless a property was paid for in silver or gold (and often even then), the type of money used almost always was spelled out.

So what? Such monetary difficulties provide meaningful clues for the genealogist, since often the place from which the buyer came was revealed when the type of money was specified, e.g., Proclamation money (from North Carolina), Virginia money, New York gold coin, Current money of Pennsylvania, "Ten Pounds, Sterling" (English silver coin) and "receipt for 4000 lbs of Virginia sweet tobacco and cask." So, by carefully reading the words describing deed consideration you may learn where an ancestor previously lived or did business.

Locating Real Estate

Deeds also describe the location of the property, sometimes in a most complete fashion and sometimes not quite so. Read those descriptions carefully, noting all landmarks, rivers, roads, and especially any names of neighboring landowners. As always, make careful notes. Better yet, have such documents copied, and then visit the offices of the County Engineer (County Surveyor) or the Tax Assessor. If they have the time to spend with you (be sure to ask), inquire if there are enough boundary details given in that deed to permit you to locate the properties on their maps. Oftentimes there will be. If so, you will find it pleasant and most meaningful to drive out to land once owned by ancestors. You will learn much, and again family history will come to life. If you do, be sure to take photographs and always accurately plot the tract on your own maps.

Probate Records

In that section of the courthouse wherein are found the *probate records*, much more is to be learned. In some places, the courts that handle probate matters are called *Surrogate Court*, or occasionally the *Orphans Court*, the *Common Pleas Court*, the *Superior Court*, the *Supreme Court*, or the *Circuit Court*. Still other names and courts are used and found in different places. If none of those titles appear on the courthouse directory, again ask anyone employed in any of the offices where you might find the probate or death records. They will know what you are talking about and will direct you to the right office.

Whatever the names used, these courts handle matters of death, mental or legal incompetence, orphans' or children's claims, and other matters wherein the physical and mental well-being of the citizenry requires the attention, action, or protection of the court. When you arrive at the probate division or section, ask where the indexes to wills and administrations are located.

You will find that the index volumes, as the deed indexes, are divided into time periods, e.g., "Beginning to 1780", "1781 to 1940", etc., and within each of those volumes, almost always in alphabetical order, you will find the names of deceased ancestors, orphans, etc., who were the subjects of the courts' actions. In most places, within those volumes the estates will be set forth in chronological order with the alphabetical index within that volume itself directing you to the appropriate page for the person sought. As always, if you do not understand the local indexing system after carefully examining it, ask someone there if they have the time to assist you.

Estates

In the estates volumes, and usually following the names of dead persons (the *decedents*), will be found notes that set forth, summarize, and date the activities in that decedent's estate, and a number or reference to a file that will contain the original papers and proceedings - in many places called the *jacket*. Simply ask the folks working there where in the building those estate files are located, and then commence your examination of that particular file.

In the case of original papers, sometimes the clerk or other person in charge will be reluctant to permit you to use them. When that happens, be polite yet persistent, and assure them that you will be very careful and not make marks in or remove items from that file (and then so conduct yourself). If the clerks in that office stand over you while you use the original files, do not be offended. It is likely that they do so with everybody since, unfortunately, too many researchers have stolen papers from their files.

It is very important to remember that if an ancestor owned land in two or more counties, you likely will find estate proceedings for him or her in each of those counties. So, if an ancestor was a person of some wealth or is known to have dealt in land, check the surrounding counties for additional estate files and deeds to and from that person. Such supplementary estate proceedings usually were (and are) called *ancillary* administrations. If the courthouse in the county in which your ancestor lived was burned sometime in the past, such ancillary proceedings and deeds recorded in neighboring counties sometimes are among the only sources for estate and land records for that ancestor.

Nearly all persons down to now have done business or been otherwise involved in *jurisdictions* (counties and towns) other than their home town or county. Accordingly, even if an ancestor was not affluent and the courthouse did not burn, it is good to spot check the records of surrounding counties. At least look at the deed and tax records there.

Testate Death Proceedings

Back to the decedents' estates files. In such files you usually will find numerous papers and writings. When a person dies, having previously executed a will, he or she is said to have died *testate* (as opposed to *intestate*: remember both words!). In a testate death it is the will that dictates who of the heirs shall get what. Immediately after death the witnesses who signed the will are summoned to court and are asked to *prove* the will, i.e., to prove through their *testimony* that the will actually was signed and acknowledged by the decedent to be his or her will. Thereafter, the appointed *executor* (a man) or the *executrix* (a woman) *executes* - carries out - the provisions of the will and performs those duties required of him or her by law. All debts must be paid and all receivables collected, and then a *final settlement* takes place dividing and distributing the remaining assets as prescribed in the will.

The objectives of all probate activity are to finally and positively conclude all of the earthly business of the dead person, and to see to it that all of his or her worldly possessions are properly distributed to his or her creditors, legal heirs, and beneficiaries. Having accomplished those objectives, the estate is then *closed* by the court. In every one of those activities, a written record is made that has value and provides clues to the researcher.

In the Name of God Amen. I Thomas
Drake of the Parrish of Nottoway in the County of South-
ampton being of Sound & Disposing mind and Memory
(thanks be to God) Do make & ordain This my Last Will and
Testament in manner & form following revoking all other
Wills by me here tofore made

First   I Give and Devise unto my Loving Wife Anne Drake
the Bed and furniture She now lies on Also I Give her the
use of the house She now lives in During her Life or widowhood

Secondly I Give and Devise unto my Son John Drake one Negro
man Slave Named Brisco after the deced of my said wife Anne
one Buckenear Gun one large Iron Pott the largest in the
House & the Largest Trunk in the House to him & his Hiers for ever

Thirdly   I Give and Devise to my Son Thomas Drake all that
Tract or parcel of Land whereon he now Lives containing
two hundred and Thirty acres lying and being in the parrish
of Nottoway & County aforesaid firmly granted to me by
Letters of pititcon thereupon perticularly bounded to hold my
son Thomas & to his Heirs for Ever I also Give to my Son
Thomas Drake after the Deced of my said wife Anne one
Negro Girl Slave Named Sarah one feather Bed and furniture
that belongs it to him and his Hiers for Ever ———

Fourthly I give & Devise to my Son William Drake one Still Cap
and Worm and that my Said Son William Shall let my Said Son

Will from 1757

*A copy of the 1757 will of Thomas Drake, signed by him with the dis-
tinctive mark "TD." He provided that his wife should have the use of the
house and of certain of his slaves during her widowhood, following
which his children were to have the slaves.*

I Give & Devise to my Son Lazarus Drake after the Death
of my wife Anne one Negro Man Slave Named Jamminy one
one Large Pine Chist one bed & furniture

I Give & Devise to my Daughter Mary the wife of William Williams
one Side Saddle & one Small Trunk

All the rest of my Estate of what Nature or kind soever to be Equally
Devided between my three Sons Viz John Thos & Lazarus and I Desire
that my two oldest sons may Devide the rest of my Estate as above
Mentioned and I Do hereby Constitute & appoint my sons Thomas
& William my whole & Sole Executors of this my Last Will & Testament
In Witness where of I have here unto Sat ony my Seal this 3 Day
of October 1757

Signed & Seald

in the presence of

Benj.a Williams
Jacob Williams
Britten Drake

                                        his
                        Thomas   T P Drake
                                       mark

At a Court held for the County of Southampton on Thursday the
11th Day of May 1758

This Will was presented in Court by Thos Drak & William Drake
the Executors therein Named proved by Benj.a Williams & Jacob
William two of the witnesses there to & Ordered to be Recorded and on
the Motion of the said Executors who made oath according to Law
Certifica was granted them for Obtaining a Probate there of in Due
form giving Security.

                        Test
                            R T Kello C.

An Additional Acco.t Curr.t of the Estate of William Hatfield deced
By an addithional State of the said Estate — — £ 1.. 2.. 9
In obedience to an order of Court bearing date March 9th 1758

As with all other documents, very carefully examine all wills. Even more so than with deeds, the witnesses found there usually were friends, relatives, or neighbors. Incidentally, a person may die testate yet not have executed a will. How so? If death is imminent and, being aware of that immediacy, the dying person makes a) positive statements disposing of his or her property, and b) these statements are written down shortly thereafter by those who heard them, the probate courts usually will give full legal effect to such last intentions and wishes. That written document is known as a *nuncupative will*, and, as with other wills, the persons who witnessed such deathbed declarations almost always were friends, neighbors, or relatives, hence, again, their names should be carefully noted. Notice too, that the dates of nuncupative wills will be very close to the date of death.

Finally as to the wills themselves, if a person left a list, written in his own hand, of his intentions and wishes concerning to whom his assets should go, even if that document fails to meet the strict requirements of law as to witnesses, acknowledgement, and form, it still is given great weight and consideration and is known as a *holographic* will. Since, unlike in early times, all of us now have ready access to lawyers, holographic wills were more common in early times than they are now.

It is important that the researcher be aware that within the early courts records, even if the death date was not given and often it was not, usually the dates will be found upon which the will was *executed* - signed - and the date upon which it was recorded. The date of recording is not the same as the date of death. Death took place between the date of the execution of the will and the recording date. Considering that early law (as now) required that the authorities be notified of a death at the very next term of court (when it next met), the actual date of death usually can be approximated by learning from the courts' records (of which below) the date upon which the preceding session (*term*) of court ended and the date the term in which the estate was commenced began. (Courts usually were held every three months, and so often were called *quarter sessions*; they lasted from a few days to several weeks.)

So, if you find that an ancestor's will was recorded on the 10th of May, 1765, and you then learn from the court minutes that the prior term ended on April 15th of that same year, almost surely the ancestor died between those dates. Since early newspapers seldom noted the deaths of other than famous and rich folks, very often this simple calculation is the only means by which to arrive at an approximate death date. Do remember, however, that where the weather usually prohibited movement - as in New England in January - courts were lenient in enforcement of the requirement that the death be reported at the very next term. So be careful in your estimates if the recording took place in winter months; in March, for example.

Intestate Death Proceedings

As noted, if a person died without a will he or she universally is said to have died *intestate*, and an *administrator* (man) or an *administratrix* (woman) is appointed by the court to perform the same tasks as did the executor or executrix who were appointed in the will and testate death examples set out above; in both cases, under the direct

State of North Carolinia Edgcombe County
this day Mary Righland of lawfull age come
before me Amos Johnston one of Justices
for Said County and after being Duely
Sworn upon the holy Evangelist Deposeth
and Sayeth that She was at the house of
Sarah Drake Dec late of this County and
that Said Sarah Drake was then Verry Ile
and that a feew day before hir death and in
presence of Drewry Drake and his Son
Lazrus She the Said Deponant heard Said
Sarah Drake Say that it was hur will
and Desire that hur Son Drewry Drake
Should have the use of hur feather bed
bedstead & all the firneture belonging to the
Bed until his Said Son Lazrus Drake
Came of Age and then for the Said
Bed & firneture to belong to Said Lazrus
(as She Said the bed &c was hur owne pro-
-perly) & further that the Said Sarah Drake
Desired that Said Drewry (his Son) Should
have all hur Clothes (and have as maney
of them as he Could ware but for him)
and ware them him Self and the Rest to
be Cut for the Children of Said Drewry
and it

Nuncupative Will

Part of a nuncupative will dated 1804. Here, the decedent told Mrs
Righland of her wishes and that her grandchildren were to have certain
of her clothes and two "gold rings."

supervision and control of the probate court. Where a death is intestate, the laws of *descent and distribution* set forth by the state wherein the dead person made his home (was *domiciled*) take the place of the provisions (*devises* and *bequests*) in the will in testate deaths and direct to whom the assets of the decedent should go. Such laws are said to control *intestate succession*.

Bonds, Inventories, Appraisements, and Sales

In all estate proceedings, whether testate or intestate (unless the dead person through a provision of the will or the probate court by positive action specifically waives the requirement), a *bond* must be posted. This bond must be sufficient in amount to guarantee the court and the heirs that the executor or the administrator, as the case may be, will see to it that the burial is accomplished and paid for, that all other debts are paid and the receivables collected, that the taxes are settled, that the assets of the dead person are protected from waste and distributed as required, and that the estate is closed. Such bonds are in an amount of money set by the court and are valuable to genealogists for two reasons. First, they were (and are) usually about twice what the court thought the assets of the dead person were worth, thus reflecting wealth or the lack of it, and, secondly, the names of the people posting that bond or acting as *sureties* were set forth. Those named sureties are important because nearly always the persons posting bonds or acting as sureties were known or related to the families of the decedents; there were but few professional bondsmen then.

In addition to the will and bond, of particular interest is the *inventory* (sometimes called *inventory and appraisement*) of the assets of the dead person. The inventory is a list of every asset (and its value) known to have belonged to the ancestor at the moment of death. By carefully studying that document a vivid picture of the farm or the house and furnishings may be drawn, from which one may deduce many of the daily activities of the family. One artist and researcher, after visiting the site of the farm of an early ancestor, from the remains of the foundations and buildings and the inventory of the assets found in the estate papers, was able to reconstruct and then paint a remarkable likeness of the long decayed and abandoned farm.

If there was a public sale or auction (in the early days called *sale by outcry*, or simply *outcry*) of the furniture or other property, that fact will appear in the file in the form of a list of goods sold, very often with the names of the buyers. Quite usually relatives will appear there and so reveal something of their whereabouts at the time. Such sales also reveal much about values of merchandise during that period, and once again the lives of your ancestors become more real.

Another document often found in the estate papers, usually called the *summary of debts and accounts*, reveals relationships with others previously unknown. Frequently one of the most difficult facts to ascertain is the occupation (if other than farmer) of an early ancestor. In addition to the inventory, summaries of accounts often provide clues as to those means of livelihood by naming suppliers of materials, merchants, or buyers of products.

Bill of Sale

In the early twentieth century the purchase of an automobile was of greater significance than now. The records of those sales may still be found at local courthouses.

KNOW all Men by these Presents, That *I, Jonathan Marston, of Brintwood, in the County of Rockingham, and State of Newhampshire husbandman*

For and in consideration of the sum of *Fifty five Dollars*

to Me in hand, before the delivery hereof, *Paid by David Marston of Brintwood, aforesaid Joiner*

the receipt whereof *I* do hereby acknowledge, have given, granted, bargained, sold, and released ; and by these presents do give, grant, bargain, sell, alien, release, convey and confirm to *him* the said *David Marston* heirs and assigns *all my Right, title, estate, property and Demand, of, in and unto the late Mansion Dwelling House of my late honord Father Winthrop Marston, late of Brintwood, aforesaid Deceased, situate in said Brintwood, on the home place of said Deceased* ... *belonging, that was reserve for the use of my part of said house in ... the Division, made between me and my brother Samuel Marston ...*

To have and to hold the said granted premises, with the appurtenances thereof to *him* the said *David Marston* heirs and assigns to *his and their* proper use, benefit and behoof forever : *I* hereby engaging to warrant and defend the said granted premises, against all claims or demands of any person or persons claiming by, from or under *me and my heirs and assigns*

In Witness whereof *I* have hereunto set *my* hand and seal, this *fourth* Day of *March* — Anno Domini, 180*5*

Signed, sealed and delivered
in presence of us,

Joseph Godfrey

Jonathan marston

marston

Rockingham the fourth — day of March 1805

THEN the above named *Jonathan Marston* personally appearing acknowledge the above written instrument to be *his* — voluntary act and deed before me,

Godfrey —Justice Peace.

Deed Revealing Occupation

An 1805 deed from "Jonathan Marston, husbandman" (keeper and breeder of livestock) and his wife Mary, to "David Marston, Joiner" (one who joins wood, usually for furniture). As here, many early deeds reveal the occupations of the parties.

Especially in intestate deaths, the final order of the court that distributes the assets will name all of the children or, if none, the *next of kin.* Incidentally, the expression next of kin refers to all relatives other than parents and children. Where a child has previously died and his or her children are to receive what would have been his or her share of an estate, those children also will be named and are said to take their share *per stirpes* (Latin).

In summary, by learning where an ancestor died, and examining all of his or her estate records, kinship and many interesting facts from the life of that ancestor will be learned. In addition to the names of the spouse and children, you may find the precise location where death took place ("drowned in the Blackwater," "killed by a train while crossing Keener Pike," etc.), the cause of death ("blood poisoning," "struck by lightning," etc.), the age as positively established by the court, perhaps the names of slaves, a complete list of land holdings, furniture, and other personal property owned, lists of accounts receivable and of debts, the names of neighbors and friends, and much more.

Lawsuits and Other Court Activities

In addition to the land and probate records, over the centuries many other legal activities were recorded. Since time immemorial, our courts have been called upon to formally deal with the everyday problems and conflicts by the process called *litigation* (the determinations of differences between people through the use of law and its processes). Moreover, over those same centuries our desire for continuity and an ordered society has demanded that written records be kept of the rulings of courts acting in such conflicts. Many of these records have been preserved and are of great value to you.

As the early judges, justices of the peace, magistrates, mayors, and chancellors sat hearing civil, criminal, and probate cases, they or their Clerks (or both) usually entered the rulings and final decisions made into notebooks. Further, during the course of the proceedings the judges themselves often made notes and entered rulings as to evidence, etc.

Those rulings were entered in volumes called variously *courts' minutes, courts' journals, order books,* or *courts' orders.* Note, however, that the words used to describe those entries and notations varied widely, and any given volume may have final decisions, entries, notes, doodlings, comments about evidence presented, notes as to some future event, and even the weather. Except for the recordings and transcripts by stenographers, there no longer are permanent records kept of the notes made by judges during trials, so the differences between minutes, orders, journals, and entries have disappeared. Perhaps less than half of the existing genealogical source materials have been the subject of abstract and extract work, and courts' minutes, journals, and order books surely rank prominently among the records yet to be studied.

When indexed, courts' writings were set out in the names of the parties. Most often, however, early minutes and journals were not indexed, and remain only in chronological order. Accordingly, since nearly all families were at one time or another involved in litigation, even if only as witnesses or coroners', grand, petit jury, or inquest members, it is necessary to search through those orders and minutes for the whole period of time during which an ancestor is known to have been within that county or jurisdiction. Start with those volumes covering months or years thought to include important events in the life of the ancestor. For example, if you know that an ancestor was born about 1740 and from the deed records that he first appeared buying land in 1775, it is reasonable to assume that he will appear thereafter for a considerable number of years, but not likely that he will appear much before since he was but a young man and probably had but few assets.

Reading Early English

The search through courts' records often is not an easy one, for even after *Elizabethan* style (so-called because of the influence of Queen Elizabeth I of England) written English fell into disuse during the eighteenth century (1700s), the quill pen handwriting of the early judges and Clerks often was nearly illegible. Further, the readability of those entries has not been improved by the passage of the centuries or by the poor quality ink then available in the colonies. Nevertheless, such records surely are worth the effort required to read them, and many provide real insight into the times during which your people lived, struggled, and died.

With a little practice you will be able to read early written English. Start with an extra copy of an early document so that you may make marks and notes on it, then go through the document very carefully and circle those words and letters which you do recognize. You will find that some of the letters will not be familiar to you, some examples of which are the longhand, lower case letter "s" which often was written like the letter "f" - *ƒ*; "ss", as in the name Jesse, might be written as "Jeppe" *Jeppe* , "Jefse" *Jefse* , or "Jeffe" - *Jeffe* ; "e" which often appeared like the letter "o" - *ᴑ* ; and "d" which was commonly written like the number "6" backwards - *ᕳ* . The word "and" often appeared as a simple loop - *Ϩ* ; "th" quite often was written quite like the letter "y" (called a thorn) - *y*; and "s" with a "d" loop over it - *ᵟᵟ* - very often was used for the word "said". Finally watch out for the symbol (usually called a crossed p) which appears like a complex letter "p" - *℔* , it often meaning variously "pre-" or "per-".

Frequently, common words were abbreviated (even in legal documents) by writing enough of the letters to make the word recognizable and then, over the top of those letters, placing the last or near last letter. "Alex" with "r" above for the name Alexander - *Alex̄* , and "Rich" with the "d" over for Richard - *Rich* . are but two examples. Often, even in the early twentieth century, indistinguishable flourishes were given to signatures, to the first letter of the first word, and to the last letter in the last word of a sentence or paragraph - *⌒*   *ᴣ* . In working through a document, try to ignore such marks and decorations.

By the time you finish the first reading you will have recognized many of the letters and words. Then go back and start over again, and stay with it until the meaning of the document becomes clear to you. Each re-reading will bring greater understanding, so be persistent.

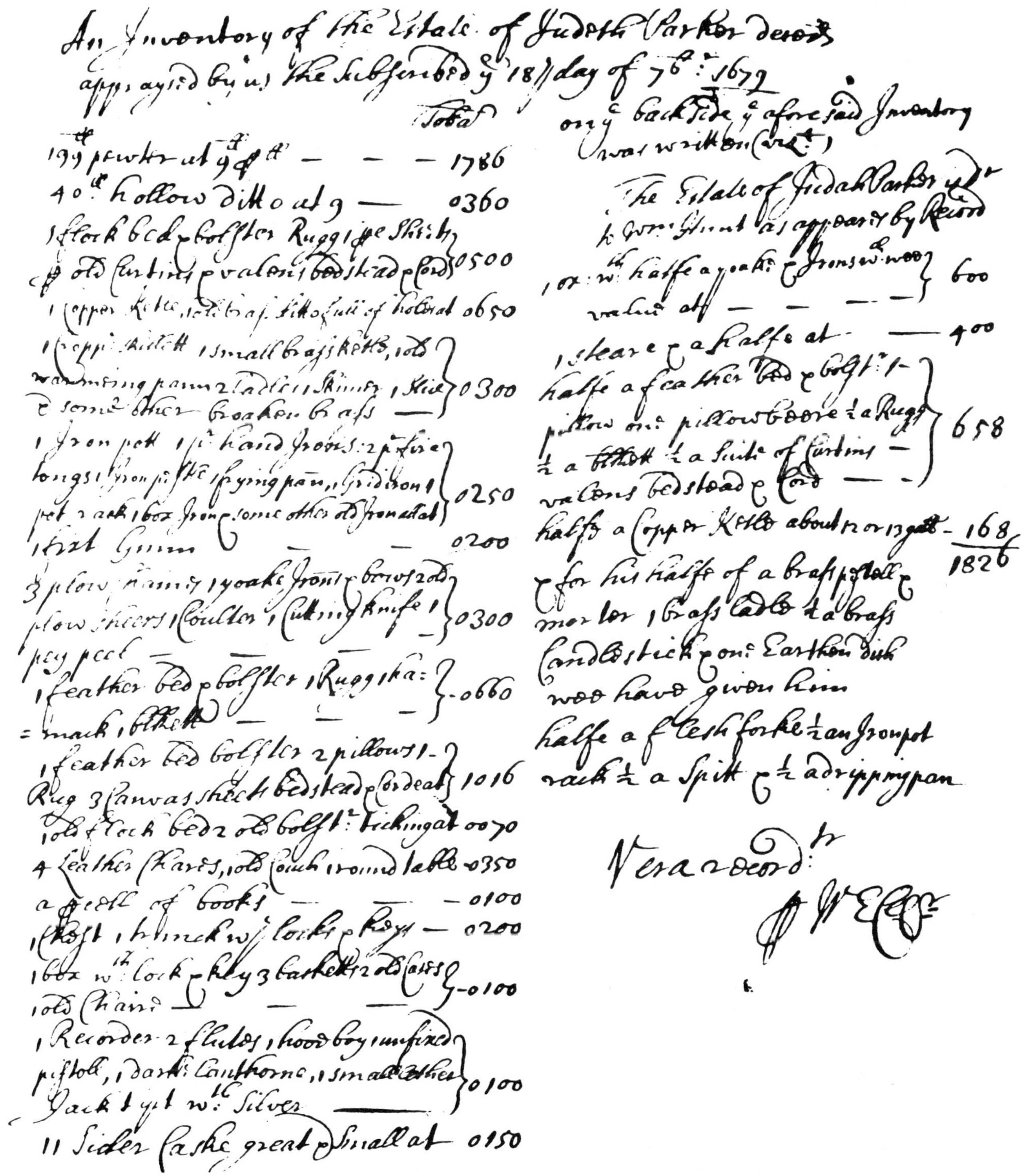

An Inventory of the Estate of Judeth Parker deceased
appraysed by us the subscribers ye 18 day of 7br: 1679

	Total
199 lb pewter at 9d p lb	1786
40 lb hollow ditto at 9	0360
1 flock bed & bolster Rugg 1 pr Sheets & old Curtins & valens bedstead & Cord	0500
1 Copper Kettle, 1 old brass ditto full of holes at	0650
1 Copper skillett 1 small brass kettle, 1 old warming pann 2 ladles 1 skimer 1 ... & some other broaken brass	0300
1 Iron pott 1 pr hand Irons 2 pr fire tongs 1 Iron pestle frying pan, 1 Gridiron 1 pot rack 1 box Iron & some other old Iron at all	0250
1 ... Gunn	0200
3 plow chaines 1 yoake Irons & brows 2 old plow sheers 1 Coulter, 1 Cutting knife 1 peg peel	0300
1 feather bed & bolster 1 Rugg 1 ka: & mack 1 blkett	0660
1 feather bed bolster 2 pillows 1 Rug 3 Canvas sheets bedstead & Cord at all	1016
1 old flock bed 2 old bolst: ticking at	0070
4 Leather Chares, 1 old Couch 1 round table	0350
a pcell of books	0100
1 Chest 1 trunck w/ locks & keys	0200
1 box wth lock & key 3 baskets 2 old Cases 1 old Chaire	0100
1 Recorder 2 flutes, 1 hoodboy 1 unfixed pistoll, 1 dark Lanthorne, 1 small other Jack & yt wth Silver	0100
11 Sider Caske great & Small at	0150

on ye back side ye aforesaid Inventory was written (viz)

The Estate of Judah Parker ... to Wm Hunt as appears by Record

10 a: wth halfe a yeak & Irons w... value at	600
1 steare & a halfe at	400
halfe a feather bed & bolst: 1 pillow one pillowbeere & a Rugg & a blkett & a suite of Curtins valens bedstead & Cord	658
halfe a Copper Kettle about 12 or 13 gall	168
	1826

& for his halfe of a brass pestell & morter, 1 brass ladle & a brass Candlestick & one Earthen dish wee have given him halfe a flesh forke & an Iron pot rack & a Spitt & ½ a drippingpan

Vera Record:

Wm E...

Early Written English

An example of early written English often encountered by the researcher. This is an estate inventory dated 18 September 1679. The inventory was done by one who was highly literate, yet not trained in calligraphy. Notice the letters a,d,e,s and ss, and the words "and" and "with."

Loose Papers

Often in the courthouses will be found groups of what are usually known as "loose papers." These are the miscellaneous pleadings (legal statements submitted by lawyers to courts), exhibits, documents, and memoranda which were a part of the early lawsuits, or simply were left at the courthouse. As now, such papers usually were not thrown away lest they should later prove to be needed by someone, yet often were stored in a quite haphazard manner. Loose papers usually are open to the public, however, as the name suggests, they are unbound and generally have no particular order or index. Still, the time spent looking through such loose materials will be amply rewarded if you come across an ancestor's signature, lawsuit, receipt, or affidavit.

Likewise, to be found in all courthouses are some record books which over the years have been kept on a shelf of miscellaneous materials. There, often you will find a surveyor's notebook, a school board ledger, minutes of county commissioner's meetings, health records, and no telling what else. Examine these materials, and if any fall within the time period in which you are searching, look through them thoroughly. Your family well may be there.

Similarly, early Clerks and Registrars of deeds often were not sure where a particular document should be filed or recorded, yet knew that such materials should be preserved. In those instances, such papers were often filed in the *Miscellaneous Records*, and have a separate index aptly called the *Miscellaneous Index* that will list the involved parties in alphabetical order. Always check it carefully for the time periods of your ancestors.

Naturalization Records

As we have seen, until we became a nation at the close of the American Revolution most of our people considered themselves to be, and indeed were, English men and women. At the close of the American Revolution almost all those who lived here were deemed to be citizens, however most who came after were not.

So it was that it became important to our government that new arrivals also be turned into Americans. The process of becoming a citizen was and still is known as *naturalization*. Both one's *Intent To Be Naturalized* and the naturalization itself were supposed to be filed and accomplished within the jurisdiction in which the new citizen (or citizen-to-be) lived, thereby providing the local civil, criminal, and taxing authorities with knowledge of that immigrant's presence.

Accordingly, you may find the naturalization of an ancestor in the records of either the local courts, or in those of the Federal court system, or both, or neither. If the indexes do not reveal a naturalization for an ancestor who you believe surely was there, ask the local court clerk for help in locating such records. They will tell you whether the same are likely to be found within their records, or direct you to that Federal courthouse where you may find them. At times, such records will be found locally in the Miscellaneous Index or even in the deed records, and in those seaport cities through

"Loose Paper"

Here is an example of an interesting 1760 "Loose Paper." Hunt wanted to build a grist mill and knew that by so doing he would cause water to back up over the lands of others. The men named found that Parker thereby would be harmed and assessed his damages at ten shillings "Current Money." Notice that we now know a lot about the event, something of Parker and Hunt, the names of some of those who lived nearby, and that the named assessors all were literate.

which many immigrants came the Clerks of the Courts sometimes have created rather complete indexes of such people.

Be aware that naturalization records usually contain only non-specific references to an area of origin, the person's name, and the date he or she was naturalized (or filed an Intent to be Naturalized). Naturalization records quite usually do not contain birth dates nor the names of parents, spouses, or children, nor will you usually find the names of the ships by which they came here.

Mention was made of the Federal Court system. Their records are nearly identical in form to those kept by the states' courts, however are wholly different as to the content (activities, litigation, and participants), and they maintain almost no records concerning local government and no deed or mortgage records. So what may be found there? Their records of lawsuits (including those involving income taxes), criminal activities, and Federal juries, both grand and petit, are superb. Simply go to the local U.S. Post Office and inquire where the Federal Courthouse is for your area of search; there are two or more for most states and at least one in every state.

Tax Records

Lastly, yet surely not least, are the tax records to be found in every courthouse, state or Federal. These are extremely valuable sources since they reflect ownership of assets (and incidental thereto, wealth or absence of the same). Since the earliest times, governments have taxed (tithed), sought to tax, or exempted from taxation the assets of all citizens who could be identified or located. Hence, even if an ancestor owned no real estate, he or she may have owned (and, for that matter, probably did own) some personal property (a cow perhaps) upon which a tax was assessed or at least considered. Accordingly, that person likely will be found in a tax record someplace. Moreover, as to the very poor, the personal property tax lists (*tax rolls*) may be the only records to be found. Indeed, if an ancestor owned or leased no real estate, or lived out on the edge of settlement, there may not have been even an administration of his or her estate, and so no record of that life or death may appear except that which may be found in the tax books.

When searching tax records remember that the terms personal property and personalty both refer to that group of assets which consists of all property other than real property. Personal property taxes usually were assessed on an annual basis and were levied against all men who were of age (as seen, not necessarily eighteen or twenty one years old) and all women who were widows or single and had assets (sometimes called by the French *femme sole*).

Since such levies were annual, one often may trace an ancestor over a considerable number of years, and just as when that person no longer appears you may presume he or she either died or moved away, you may presume that during those years before the first appearance he or she either was not of age or had not yet arrived. Thus you will have gained knowledge of yet more events in the life of an ancestor.

Remember that the early enumerations of tithables also were tax lists, the word *tithe* having come from ancient English law and its requirements that increase from the land - crops, etc. - and the fruits of one's labors might be assessed for tax purposes. So too were *polls* (that term simply meaning lists of persons by count), and a *poll tax* sometimes was called a *head tax* since it was levied against all who were in a particular class or group of people. Incidentally, of all levies the poll taxes were the most despised, especially by the poor or nearly so, since, unless specifically excluded, these taxes often were levied against all, even infants, old widows, and the disabled or infirm, without regard to their ability to pay.

Those who were considered *tithable* - required to pay a tax - varied from time to time, however generally it may be said that males over sixteen, all slaves, and all Free Blacks or other Free Persons of Color fell within these categories, and that women (again, unless femme sole) were not tithable. Notice that if an ancestor is found with three tithables shown within his household (three persons chargeable to him for tax purposes), you have no clues as to the number of females within the household. To approximate the number of women and girls in the house, since their numbers usually were about equal to the numbers of men plus the live-ins (men did not live as long as women), simply double the number of tithables listed other than the slaves.

Most importantly, tax lists reveal the presence of an ancestor in a certain geographical area or jurisdiction, and tell you something of his or her belongings and household - wealth. Caution: the numbers designating the unnamed tithables or those subject to the poll taxes that are listed with the names of ancestors again may be misleading, since, as we have learned, there may be apprentices and others for whom an ancestor was taxable yet who were not immediate family. Thus, it should not be presumed that unnamed yet taxed persons were kin to the head of household.

Very early local tax records, if they have not been removed to a local library, historical society, or the states' archives, usually will be found in the Clerks' of Courts offices, with the deed records, or in the offices of the county Tax Assessors. If you do not find them, ask at the Assessor's office; they will know where they are if they still exist.

Nearly always, as with deeds, tax record indexes are divided into time periods, and then within each time period the taxpayers will be set forth in alphabetical order. With these records, as with all others, if you can not locate the index among the materials or, when found, can not figure out how to use it, ask someone in that office. They will help, so utilize these fine sources.

Good Genealogy Manners

A word should be said concerning conduct in libraries and courthouses. In all your activities you should both exercise and encourage others to use good genealogy manners. Too many folks are noisy, inconsiderate, and demanding while researching. Especially in the courthouses, the others working with those records are at the task of earning a livelihood, and in consideration of those efforts we should work quietly, without family chatter, and seek to learn in advance of those times and days during

District # 1	4 Sept.		# 229 BATY (cont)			
			Lane	17	f	Tenn +
# 222			Dibra	15	f	" +
Joshua OWENS	52	m SC	Martin	13	m	" +
Mary	46	f Ky	John	10	m	" +
John	24	m Tenn	Emeline	8	f	"
Abby	21	f "	Rhoda	3	f	"
Elias	18	m "				
Jas	17	m "	# 230			
Cyntha	13	f "	David BATY *Th.*	33	m	Tenn =
Winna	8	f "	Ava *Avery ?? ?*	29	f	"
			Charlotte - m stephens ?	10	f	" +
# 223			Jas	7	m	" +
Geo OWENS	56	m NC	Clayburn	5	m	"
Sally	50	f Tenn =	Harvey *Sheriff*	2	m	"
Susa	21	f " =				
Geo	20	m " +	# 231			
Lane	19	f Pa	Austin CHOAT	55	m	Va =
Thos	17	m Tenn +	Elizabeth	49	f	"
Andrew	15	m " +	Jacob	24	m	Tenn
Samuel	13	m " +	Sally	18	f	"
Charlotte	11	f " +	Ann	15	f	"
Sarah	7	f "	Celia	13	f	" +
Sarah	90	f NC	John	10	m	" +
			Christopher	8	m	" +
# 224			Denna	4	f	"
Anderson HOGG	70	f NC =				
Elizabeth	50	f Tenn =	# 232			
			Jas ADKISON	20	m	Tenn
# 225			Nancy	22	f	" =
William WOODS	21	m Tenn	Mary	1/12	f	"
Catherine	23	f "				
Cintha *Cynthia*	2	f "	# 233			
Mary	10/12	f "	Geo CHOAT	29	m	Tenn =
			Linda	25	f	" =
# 226			Malissa	6	f	"
John BATY *1859*	65	m Pa =	Lusy	4	f	"
Betsy	52	f Tenn =	Jas	2	m	"
Geo *7*	18	m "	Jacob	1	m	"
Jas	15	m "				
Thos	5	m "	# 234			
			John WINEHAM	35	m	Tenn
# 228			Isaac	30	m	"
Jackson STEPHENS	21	m Tenn*=	Eliza	23	f	"
Charlotte	20	f " *	Geo	1	m	Tenn
Elizabeth BATY	24	f Tenn	Jas BEAN	27	m	Tenn =
Armilda "	10/12	f "	Sarah "	25	f	"
			John "	5	m	"
# 229			Wm "	2	m	"
William BATY *1850 36 1794*	56	m Tenn				
Martha	53	f " =	# 235			
Sally	24	f " =	Wilburn HOGG	42	m	Ky
Nancy	20	f "	Rachel	40	f	Tenn
Geo (cont)	18	m " +	Vardernan	19	m	Ky +
			Solomon	15	m	Tenn +
			Lewis (cont)	17	m	" +

"Errors Corrected" by Past Researchers

Here is a page from a transcription of the 1850 Decennial Census of Tennessee. Note the inappropriate comments made in the transcription by past researchers.

which the schedules are particularly tedious. Simply call ahead and inquire as to rules, if any, and of the times which are the most convenient to that office to have you there. You will be amazed at how much better you will be treated and how much more help will be available to you by reason of that small courtesy on your part.

Care of Records

The folks at the courthouse are custodians of archives which often are very fragile and old. One of their jobs is to care for and preserve such materials. As researchers we too have an obligation to act in such a fashion that future generations may enjoy our hobby. Too often, family researchers, having learned that such records are public, have been abusive and have not exercised care in handling the old books and documents. Never tear or make marks in books and records, and, unless the rule directs you to not re-shelve books, always put them back exactly where you found them.

If you find that someone before you has attempted to "correct" an entry in a public record, be skeptical; the correction is only as reliable as was the person who made it (and you do not even know who it was). If you do uncover an error in the recorded materials, do not add to the problem by writing in your own version or correction. Simply make your own notes, describe the error in your *citations* - references - in order that those who later search will not have the same difficulty, and point out the error to the folks in that office. They may or may not be interested in such help, so do not be disappointed if they seem unconcerned.

At the risk of being repetitious, let us say again: You must not be intimidated by the mass of records in the courthouses. The folks there - and their many predecessors - have been at the business of preserving and cataloguing records for a thousand years and more. Their methods are as sound and easy to use as man's inventiveness over the centuries could permit. Only now, with computer technology at hand, will changes of substance and method be made in indexing. So go in, ask for help if you need it, and enjoy the wealth of materials waiting there for you. Too many of us have not.

Throughout every aspect of your search, when you find interesting and important materials, whether during your interviews, at the courthouses, in the libraries, or wherever, always make copies in order that others of your family or friends may enjoy the same records as much as you did. Further, and very important, frequently many years later a re-examination of an old copy will awaken you to an entirely different interpretation from that originally made. In that regard, always be willing to give up old ideas and conclusions, no matter how long you may have held them. We all have had to abandon old notions from time to time.

Writing About Your Family

One day you likely will want to write of your family in a style that will be interesting to others; most of us do. So it is that while the writing of family history is beyond the scope of this handbook, it is necessary that a few words be said about that matter.

Furniture and Stock of what Nature or kind
So Ever During her Life or widow hood also I give
her the use of all my Negros During her Life or
widowhood

Secondly: after the Death of my wife Sarah I give unto my
Sun Jesse Five pound proc as Soon as it Can be
Raisd opt of the Estate as I have given him what
I think proper beforehand

Thirdly: I give unto my Daughter An wife of beniamin
Mosley after the Death of my wife Sarah
Twenty Shillings proc as Soon as it Can be Raisd
out of the Estate

Forthly: I give unto my Sun william Drake all my
Tools Belonging To my Trade & to he Shall Let
my Sons Daniel Drake hand himes have the
the Liberty to work with the Tools if they Require
it

Fifthly: after the Death of my wife Sarah I give unto
my Sun Drewry Drake the plantation I now
Live on ~~[struck through]~~ But on Case
my Sun Drewry Should Dey without Ishshow Then
my Sun hines Drake to the plantation and if
my Sun hines Should Dey without Isshey Then
it is my Desire my Sun Daniel Should possess
the plantation whereon I now Live

Lastly: all the Rest and Remainer of my Estate of what
Nature or kind So Ever to be Equally Devided
between my Six Children william Daniel Sally
Hines Elezabeth and Drewry Excepting one
Negro Boy Cald Coffe I Leave to my Sun Drewry
Drake but in Case my Sun Drewry Should
Dey without Heir Then the Negro Boy Cald Coffe
to be Brought into the Rest of the Estate

174

Legibility

The family historian often encounters writings that are difficult to read.
Nevertheless, we must strive to understand what is found. In this 1774
will the testator states that he has six children and then names them
all, including the names of the husbands of his daughters; a very
valuable bit of proof of lineage despite the near illegibility.

Writing takes practice; a lot of it. Such magnificence in historical writings as displayed by the likes of Churchill, Bruce, Fiske, Foote, etc., came only after many years of effort and practice. They were not born with that talent, nor were you, and to be prepared to one day undertake such an effort, however small, you must commence now.

How? Every time you learn a new fact or gain another reference force yourself to write it in sentence form; not later, do it right then. And the lined paper kept in the binder with your family group or unit charts is a good place to enter such sentences. As an example, having known of her death, when you learned of our imaginary Grace McCart's birth, you should have entered those facts not as "Grace McCart, b. 1871, d. Mar. 1, 1950," rather you should have taken the time to write "Grandmother Grace McCart was born in Illinois, probably in 1871, and died there at the age of seventy-nine on March 1, 1950." Then, following that sentence, in an abbreviated form, you should have written the source of that information - e.g., "1880 Census, Illinois, Smith County, Roll 184, page 68, residence 312, family 382." By requiring such simple sentences of yourself, soon you will be writing multiple sentences and then paragraphs. Finally, an assembling of those paragraphs one day will provide a basis for chapters concerning those branches of your family.

In addition, at once you should commence the effort to gather together all mementos, letters, documents, photos, and copies of materials which have to do with your family, wherever they may be. How? Most family collections result from nothing more than requests of relatives for mementos which they no longer want or need. You will be surprised at the materials that relatives will give you simply because you are interested, and nobody in their direct line is.

One researcher, while interviewing an elderly great uncle, asked if he might have any family items of which the uncle had duplicates or did not need. In response, the old man went to another room, returned with a small box, and told the researcher that his efforts were very much appreciated and since none of the uncle's children had shown any similar interest, while he had no duplicates, the interviewer could have and keep the Civil War discharge certificate of his father, the old veteran's medallions and soldier's hymnal, and the original War of 1812 widow's pension papers of that old soldier's mother! Needless to say, that researcher never again hesitated to ask for items no longer needed. So, after telling them that you have undertaken to gather together the mementos of the family for the benefit of all and that great care will be taken of all mementos, photos, etc., ask all relatives for any family items which they no longer need or want.

About Computers

Lastly, since more and more libraries and fellow genealogist are using computers, it is necessary that a few words be said about these incredible time savers. The effort saved is truly amazing; the ease with which corrections may be made is equally wondrous; the speed with which you may copy materials for forwarding to others surpasses any technology ever before at hand; and your capacity to write of your history is expanded to the utmost degree. The use of such devices is no more difficult to learn than it is to learn to use a modern typewriter; programs are available which have incorporated the very best of our methods; and, finally, short courses in the use of computers are available in virtually every community.

Even though most of the recognized genealogists of today undertook this hobby with no inkling of such devices - indeed, even without electric typewriters - in this instance what was good enough for grandpa is not good enough for you, and we very much recommend that you expend the little time necessary to learn something of the use of modern word processors. The rewards will be far beyond your expectations.

Conclusion

The gathering and study of family history is not only worthwhile, it provides an inner reward and an intellectual challenge seldom found in any other hobby. Not only will you become a detective and an amateur historian, you will learn and appreciate much of human nature and even more about how your own people lived (and died).

As a result of our research efforts, most of us have developed a deep regard and abiding interest in some certain family member or line, which interest has driven us to seek out every last word and scrap of evidence concerning those lives. All of us have come to have a deep respect for the enormous effort that was demanded of and accomplished by our pioneer ancestors. So will you.

They were a strong people - those who struggled through the wars, sometimes through destitution and often through hard times, through the filth of the cities, the snakes and mosquitoes of the Carolina swamps, the heat of south Alabama and the terrible cold of northern Vermont, the long, long, long years - and a good thing it was too; they had an America to build and frontiers to conquer at every turn. Frontiers in science, in medicine, in the arts, in exploration, in every field of endeavor. Perhaps it could not be better said than by Churchill:

> *We have not traveled all this way across the centuries - across the oceans, across the mountains, across the prairies - because we were made of sugar candy.*

(to Canadian Commons, December, 1940)

Good Luck, and may we meet someplace, sometime.

Appendix 1

Forms

This section contains a number of genealogical forms discussed in this book. The first form is a Pedigree Chart, the second is a Family Unit Chart and after that follow eleven census forms, from 1790 to 1920, which will assist you in your research. To use any of the forms, simply make as many copies as you need.

For inclusion in this book the original forms had to be reduced, so when you make copies you might want to enlarge them again (approximately 110-115%) to improve readability and ease of use.

PEDIGREE CHART

Compiler _____

Address _____

_____

Date _____

The first person on this chart is the same person as No. _____ on chart No. _____.

CHART NO. ◯

KEY
ca   about
cont.   continuation
b   date of birth
p b   place of birth
m   date of marriage
p.m   place of marriage
d   date of death
p.d   place of death

Record dates as day, month, year
  4 July 1776
Record places as city (county) state
  Chicago (Cook) Illinois

b.
p.b.
m.
p.m.
d.
p.d.

b.
p.b.
m.
p.m.
d.
p.d.

b.
p.b.
m.
p.m.
d.
p d

b.
p.b.
m.
p.m.
d.
p.d.

b.
p.b.
d.
p.d.

b.
p.b.
m.
p.m.
d.
p.d.

b.
p.b.
d.
p.d.

b
p.b.
d.
p.d.

cont.
chart
◯

b.
p.b.
m.
p.m.
d.
p.d.

cont.
chart
◯

b.
p.b.
d.
p.d.

cont.
chart
◯

b.
p.b.
m.
p.m.
d.
p.d.

cont.
chart
◯

b.
p.b.
d.
p.d.

cont.
chart
◯

b.
p.b.
m.
p.m.
d.
p.d.

cont.
chart
◯

b.
p.b.
d.
p.d.

cont.
chart
◯

b.
p.b.
m.
p.m.
d.
p.d.

cont.
chart
◯

b.
p.b.
d.
p.d.

National Genealogical Society, 1921 Sunderland Pl. N.W., Washington, D.C. 20036

PEDIGREE CHART

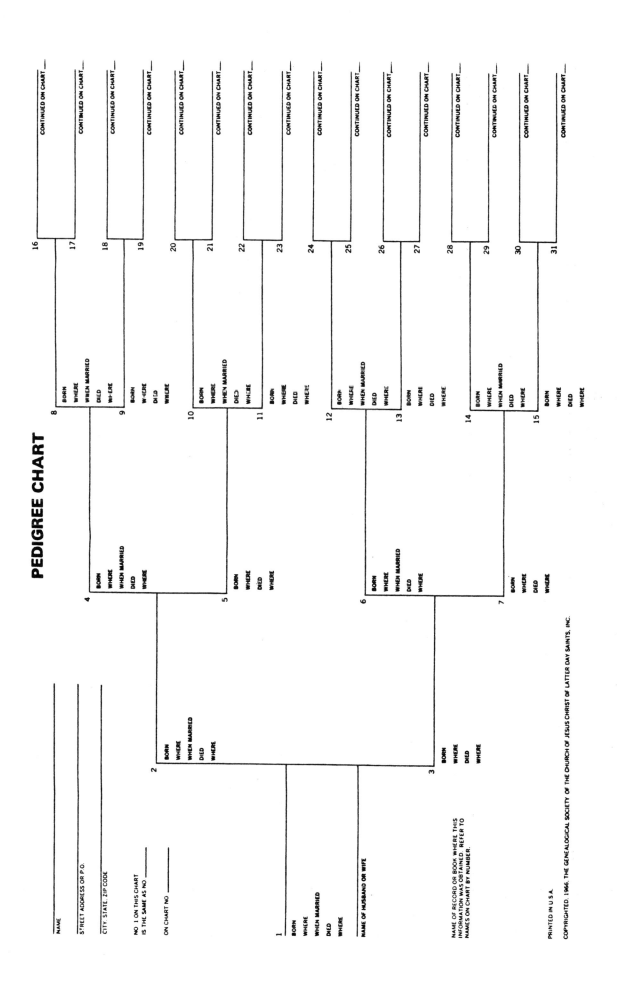

NAME

STREET ADDRESS OR P.O.

CITY, STATE, ZIP CODE

NO. 1 ON THIS CHART
IS THE SAME AS NO _____

ON CHART NO _____

1

BORN
WHERE
WHEN MARRIED
DIED
WHERE

NAME OF HUSBAND OR WIFE

NAME OF RECORD OR BOOK WHERE THIS
INFORMATION WAS OBTAINED. REFER TO
NAMES ON CHART BY NUMBER.

PRINTED IN U.S.A.

2
BORN
WHERE
WHEN MARRIED
DIED
WHERE

3
BORN
WHERE
DIED
WHERE

4
BORN
WHERE
WHEN MARRIED
DIED
WHERE

5
BORN
WHERE
DIED
WHERE

6
BORN
WHERE
WHEN MARRIED
DIED
WHERE

7
BORN
WHERE
DIED
WHERE

8
BORN
WHERE
WHEN MARRIED
DIED
WHERE

9
BORN
WHERE
DIED
WHERE

10
BORN
WHERE
WHEN MARRIED
DIED
WHERE

11
BORN
WHERE
DIED
WHERE

12
BORN
WHERE
WHEN MARRIED
DIED
WHERE

13
BORN
WHERE
DIED
WHERE

14
BORN
WHERE
WHEN MARRIED
DIED
WHERE

15
BORN
WHERE
DIED
WHERE

16 CONTINUED ON CHART ___

17 CONTINUED ON CHART ___

18 CONTINUED ON CHART ___

19 CONTINUED ON CHART ___

20 CONTINUED ON CHART ___

21 CONTINUED ON CHART ___

22 CONTINUED ON CHART ___

23 CONTINUED ON CHART ___

24 CONTINUED ON CHART ___

25 CONTINUED ON CHART ___

26 CONTINUED ON CHART ___

27 CONTINUED ON CHART ___

28 CONTINUED ON CHART ___

29 CONTINUED ON CHART ___

30 CONTINUED ON CHART ___

31 CONTINUED ON CHART ___

FAMILY UNIT CHART

x = Direct
Ancestⱼ
√ = LDS Temple
Ord. Compl.

PREPARED BY _____   DATE _____

HUSBAND

	DATE -- DAY, MONTH, YEAR	CITY	OCCUPATION COUNTY	STATE or COUNTRY	ANCESTRAL CHART #	FAMILY UNIT #
Born						
Christened						
Married						
Died						
Buried						
FATHER						
MOTHER						

OTHER WIVES:

WIFE maiden name

Born				
Christened				
Died				
Buried				
FATHER				
MOTHER				

OTHER HUSBANDS:

X	SEX	CHILDREN	BIRTH			BIRTHPLACE			DATE OF FIRST MARRIAGE		DATE OF DEATH		
√	M/F	Living, Adopted, Dead—In Order of Birth	Day	Month	Year	City	County	St./Cty.	Name of Spouse	City	County	State/Country
		1										
		2										
		3										
		4										
		5										
		6										
		7										
		8										
		9										
		10										
		11										
		12										
		13										
		14										

1790 CENSUS – UNITED STATES

State _____

Call No. _____ .

County	City	Page	Head of Family	Free White Males		Free White Females	All Other Persons	Slaves
				16 & up incl. head of families	Under 16	Incl. head of family		

1800–1810 CENSUS – UNITED STATES

State _____ County _____ City _____ Call No. _____

Page	Head of Family	Free White Males					Free White Females					All Others	Slaves	Remarks
		Under 10	10–16	16–26	26–45	45 & Over	Under 10	10–16	16–26	26–45	45 & Over			

1820 CENSUS — UNITED STATES

State _____ County _____ City _____ Call No. _____

Page	Head of Family	Free White Males						Free White Females					Foreigners not naturalized	Agriculture	Commerce	Manufactures	Free Colored	Slaves	Remarks
		Under 10	10–16	16–18	16–26	26–45	45 and over	Under 10	10–16	16–26	26–45	45 and over							

1830 - 1840 CENSUS – UNITED STATES

State _____ County _____ City _____ Call No. _____

Page	Head of Family	Free White Males														Free White Females														Slaves	Free Colored	Foreigners not naturalized.
		Under 5	5-10	10-15	15-20	20-30	30-40	40-50	50-60	60-70	70-80	80-90	90-100	Over 100	Under 5	5-10	10-15	15-20	20-30	30-40	40-50	50-60	60-70	70-80	80-90	90-100	Over 100			

1850 CENSUS   UNITED STATES

State _____ County _____ Township _____ Town _____ Call No.

Page	Dwelling Number	Family Number	Names	Age	Sex	Color	Occupation, etc.	Value - Real Estate	Birthplace	Married within year	School within year	Cannot read or write	Enumeration Date	Remarks

1860 CENSUS UNITED STATES

State _____ County _____ Town/Township _____ P.O. _____ Call No. _____

Page	Dwelling No.	Family No.	Names	Age	Sex	Color	Occupation, etc.	Value - Real Estate	Value - Personal Property	Birthplace	Married in Year	School in Year	Can't Read or Write	Enumeration Date	Remarks

1870 CENSUS – UNITED STATES

State _____ County _____ Town _____ Township _____ P.O. _____ Call No. _____

Page	Dwelling No.	Family No.	Names	Age	Sex	Color	Occupation, etc.	Value - Real Estate	Value - Personal property	Birthplace	Father Foreign born	Mother Foreign born	Month born in year	Month married in year	School in Year	Can't Read or Write	Eligible to vote	Date of Enumeration

1880 CENSUS – UNITED STATES

State ___

County ___

Township ___

Town ___

Call No. ___

Page	Dwelling No.	Family No.	Names	Color	Sex	Age prior to June 1st	Month of birth, if born in census yr.	Relationship to head of house	Single	Married	Widowed	Divorced	Married in census year	Occupation	Miscellaneous Information	Cannot read or write	Place of birth	Place of birth of father	Place of birth of mother	Enumeration Date

1900 CENSUS

Microfilm ____
Roll No. ____

State ____

County ____

Town/Township ____

Date ____

Supv. Dist. No. ____

Enum. Dist. No. ____

Sheet No. ____

Page No. ____

LOCATION				NAME	PERSONAL DESCRIPTION									NATIVITY			CITIZENSHIP			OCCUPATION		EDUCATION					
Street	House No.	Dwelling No.	Family No.	of each person whose place of abode on June 1, 1900, was in this family	Relation to head of family	Color	Sex	Month of birth	Year of birth	Age	Single, married, widowed, divorced	No. of years married	Mother of how many children	Number of these children living	Place of birth	Place of birth of father	Place of birth of mother	Year of immigration to U.S.	No. of years in U.S.	Naturalization	Occupation	No. of months not employed	Attended school (months)	Can read	Can write	Can speak English	Home owned or rented	Home owned free or mortgaged	Farm or house

1910 Census – United States

State _____ County _____ Township or other Division of County _____

Enumeration Date _____ Roll _____ Sheet _____ Dist. _____

LOCATION			NAME	RELATION	PERSONAL DESCRIPTION									BIRTHPLACE		
House number city or town	Number of dwelling house	Number of family	Of each person living in this family on April 15, 1910 (Include every person living on April 15, 1910. Omit children born since April 15, 1910	Relationship of the person to the head of the family	Sex	Color or race.	Age at last birthday.	Single, married, widowed, or divorced	Number of yrs. present marr.	Mother of how many children — Number born	Mother of how many children — Number Now living			Place of birth of this person.	Place of birth of father of this person.	Place of birth of mother of this person.

Line: 1, 2, 3, 4, 5, 6, 7, 8

CITIZENSHIP		OCCUPATION							EDUCATION			OWNERSHIP OF HOME						REMARKS
Year of immi-gration to U S	Naturalized or Alien	Speak English; or, if not, language spoken.	Trade or profession or particular kind of work done by person, as spinner, salesman, laborer, etc.	General nature of industry, business, or establishment in which person works, as cotton mill, dry goods store, farm, etc.	Whether an employer, employe or work-ing own account	If employee — Out of work on April 15, 1910	If employee — Weeks out of work during year 1909		Able to read?	Able to write?	Attended school any time since Sept. 1, 1909	Owned or rented	Owned free or mortgaged	Farm or house	Number of farm schedule	Whether survivor Union, Confederate Army or Navy	Whether blind (both eyes) / Whether deaf and dumb	

Line: 1, 2, 3, 4, 5, 6, 7, 8

SHEET #_____ **A**

DEPARTMENT OF COMMERCE-BUREAU OF THE CENSUS

FOURTEENTH CENSUS OF THE UNITED STATES: 1920-POPULATION

STATE_____   SUPERVISOR'S DISTRICT_____

COUNTY_____   ENUMERATION DISTRICT_____

TOWNSHIP OR OTHER DIVISION OF COUNTY_____

NAME OF INCORPORATED PLACE_____ WARD OF CITY_____

FILM SERIES T 625:   ROLL_____   NAME OF INSTITUTION_____

ENUMERATOR_____ ENUMERATED ON THE_____DAY OF_____1920.

PLACE OF ABODE				NAME	REL.	TENURE		PERSONAL DESCRIPTION				CITIZENSHIP			EDUCATION		
Street, avenue, road, etc.	House number or farm	Number of dwelling house in order of visitation.	Number of family in order of visitation.	of each person whose place of abode on January 1, 1920, was in this family. Enter surname first, then given and middle initial if any. Omit children born since January 1, 1920.	To head of household.	Home owned or rented	If owned, free or mortgaged.	Sex.	Color or race.	Age at last birthday.	Single, married, widowed, or divorced	Year of Immigration to the United States.	Naturalized or alien.	If naturalized, year of naturalization.	Attended school any time since 1 Sept 1919	Whether able to read.	Whether able to write.
1	2	3	4	5	6	7	8	9	10	11	12	13	14	15	16	17	18
				1													
				2													
				3													
				4													
				5													
				6													
				7													
				8													
				9													
				10													
				11													
				12													
				13													
				14													
				15													

FILM READ AT_____

BY_____ DATE_____

NOTES

	NATIVITY AND MOTHER TONGUE Place of birth of each person and parents of each person enumerated. If born in the United States, give the state or territory. If foreign born, give the place of birth and, in addition, the mother tongue.						Whether able to speak English.	OCCUPATION		Employer, salary or wage worker, or working as own account.	Number of farm schedule.
	PERSON		FATHER		MOTHER			Trade, profession, or particular kind of work done, as *spinner, salesman, laborer, etc.*	Industry, business, or establishment in which at work, as *cotton mill, dry goods store, farm, etc.*		
	Place of Birth	Mother Tongue	Place of Birth	Mother Tongue	Place of Birth	Mother Tongue					
	19	20	21	22	23	24	25	26	27	28	29
1											
2											
3											
4											
5											
6											
7											
8											
9											
10											
11											
12											
13											
14											
15											

Appendix 2

The National Archives

As mentioned in Chapter 2, page 22 and onwards, the researcher can procure by mail copies of such valuable records as veteran or widow pension applications, land-bounty warrants and more from the National Archives. To request a search of the Archives you will need to use form NATF-80. To receive form NATF-80 free of charge write to the following address:

General Reference Branch (NNRG-P)
National Archives and Records Administration
7th and Pennsylvania Avenue NW.
Washington, DC 20408

You will need to fill out a separate NATF-80 form for each individual whose records you want searched, so order several. Your forms will arrive complete with all information you will need on how to fill them out, how to pay etc. The types of records that can be searched are:

Pension Application Files

These are the most useful records for genealogical research and contain most complete information on a man's military career. The National Archives recommend that you first request the Pension Application Files.

The Pension Application Files are based on Federal (*not State*) service before World War I. Pensions based on Confederate service were authorized by some southern states but until 1959 not by the Federal Government.

Bounty-land Warrant Files

Request when no pension file exists. If the veteran's service was during the Revolutionary war, bounty-land warrant files have been consolidated with pension application files and can be obtained by requesting the pension files only.

Bounty-land warrant files are based again on Federal, and not State, service before 1856. The information in the files is similar to that in pension application files. Additionally these files usually give the veteran's age and place of residence at the time of application.

Military Service Records

These only rarely contain family information. The Military Service Records are based on service in one of the following United States military organizations:
- Army: officers who served before June 30, 1917
  enlisted men who served before October 31, 1912.
- Navy: officers who served before 1903
  enlisted men who served before 1886.

- Marine Corps: officers who served before 1896
                enlisted men who served before 1905.
- Confederate Armed Forces:
                officers and enlisted men who served between 1861 and 1865.
- Volunteers who fought in various wars from the Revolutionary war through the Philippine Insurrection, covering the period from 1775 to 1902.

For records relating to service in World War I, II, or later, write to:
National Personnel Records Center (Military Records)
NARA
9700 Page Boulevard
St. Louis, MO 63132

Census Records

The National Archives does not search census records, but it can provide copies of specific pages of Federal population census schedules. Use form NATF-81 to request the copies.

Minimum information you will need to provide:
- name of the individual listed
- page number
- census year
- county and state

For the 1880 through 1910 censuses you will need to provide the enumeration district as well.

Ship Passenger Arrival Records

The National Archives has inbound Federal Ship Passenger Arrival Records. A number of these have been indexed, others have not. Use form NATF-82 to request a search of these records.

The following major indexes of passenger lists exist:

Baltimore	1820-1952
Boston	1848-1891 and 1902-1920
New Orleans	1853-1952
New York	1820-1846 and 1897-1948
Philadelphia	1800-1948
Minor ports	1820-1874 and 1890-1924

Notice that no law required that arrival records be kept for persons entering the US by land via Canada or Mexico, or for outbound ship passengers.

To have the indexes searched you will need to provide the following information:
- full name of the passenger
- port of entry
- approximate date of arrival

To have unindexed passenger lists searched you will need to supply the following minimum information:
- full name of the passenger
- name of the ship

- port of entry
- approximate date of arrival

or

- full name of the passenger
- port of embarkation
- port of entry
- exact date of arrival

For unindexed lists after 1892, you will need to provide:
- full name of passenger
- names and ages of accompanying passengers, if any
- name of the ship
- port of entry
- exact date of arrival

In addition, you can also order copies of an entire passenger list or search the records yourself (or have them searched by a representative) if they are too voluminous for the National Archives staff to search.

Naturalization Records

These are separate from passenger arrival lists. The National Archives has copies of naturalization papers for the years 1798 to 1906 for:

> Massachusetts,
> New Hampshire,
> Rhode Island,
> Maine,

in addition to original records for the District of Columbia for the years 1802 to 1926.

For information on citizenship granted elsewhere though September 26, 1906 write to the Federal, State or municipal court that issued the naturalization. For information on naturalizations after September 26, 1906, write to:

> *The Immigration and Naturalization Service*
> *Washington, DC 20536*

National Archives Regional Archives System

You may visit the following regional archives to research Federal population census records dating from 1790 to 1910. However, the regional offices do not offer the mail order photocopying service of the General Reference Branch (address at the beginning of this section) . Call for current hours of operation.

National Archives - **Alaska Region**
654 West 3rd Avenue
Anchorage, AK 99501
Phone: (907) 271-2441
Areas served: *Alaska.*

National Archives-**Central Plains Region**
2313 East Bannister Road
Kansas City, MO 64131
Phone: (816) 926-6272
Areas served: *Iowa, Kansas, Missouri, Nebraska.*

National Archives - **Great Lakes Region**
7358 South Pulaski Road
Chicago, IL 60629
Phone: (312) 581-7816
Areas served: *Illinois, Indiana, Michigan, Minnesota, Ohio, Wisconsin.*

National Archives - **Mid Atlantic Region**
9th & Market Streets, Room 1350
Philadelphia, PA 19107
Phone: (215) 597-3000
Areas served: *Delaware, Maryland, Pennsylvania, Virginia, West Virginia.*

National Archives - **New England Region**
380 Trapelo Road
Waltham, MA 02154
Phone: (617) 647-8100
Areas served: *Connecticut, Maine, Massachusetts, New Hampshire, Rhode Island, Vermont.*

National Archives - **Northeast Region**
Building 22, Military Ocean Terminal
Bayonne, NJ 07002-5388
Phone: (201) 823-7545
Areas served: *New Jersey, New York, Puerto Rico, Virgin Islands.*

National Archives - **Pacific Southwest Region**
24000 Avila Road
Laguna Niguel, CA 92677-6719
Phone: (714) 643-4241
Areas served: *Arizona; southern Californian counties of Imperial, Inyo, Kern, Los Angeles, Orange, Riverside, San Bernardino, San Diego, San Luis Obispo, Santa Barbara, Ventura; and Clark County, Nevada.*

National Archives - **Pacific Northwest Region**
6125 Sand Point Way
Seattle, WA 98115
Phone: (206) 526-6507
Areas served: *Idaho, Oregon, Washington.*

National Archives - **Pacific Sierra Region**
1000 Commodore Drive
San Bruno, CA 94066
Phone: (415) 876-9009
Areas served: *Northern California, Hawaii, Nevada (except for Clark County) , Pacific Ocean Area.*

National Archives - **Rocky Mountain Region**
Building 48, Denver Regional Center
Denver, CO 80225
Phone: (303) 236-0817
Areas served: *Colorado, Montana, North Dakota, South Dakota, Utah, Wyoming.*

National Archives - **Southeast Region**
1557 St. *Joseph Avenue*
East Point, GA 30344
Phone: (404) 763-7477
Areas served: Alabama, Georgia, Florida, Kentucky, Mississippi, North Carolina, South Carolina, Tennessee.

National Archives - **Southwest Region**
501 West Felix Street
Fort Worth, TX 76115
Phone: (817) 334-5525
Areas served: *Arkansas, Louisiana, New Mexico, Oklahoma, Texas.*

Appendix 3

Societies, Periodicals and Directories

Following are the names addresses of a few general societies and periodicals plus six directories. Addresses and prices are correct to the best of our knowledge but the reader is advised to check first.

Societies

Afro-American Historical & Genealogical Society
    P.O. Box 73086
    Washington, DC 20055

Association of Jewish Genealogical Societies
    1485 Teaneck Road
    Teaneck, NJ 07666

Board for Certification of Genealogists
    P.O. Box 19165
    Washington, DC 20036

Canadian Federation of Genealogical & Family History Societies
    40 Celtic Bay
    Winnipeg, MB
    Canada R3T 2W9

Federation of Genealogical Societies
    2324 E. Nottingham
    Springfield, MO 65804

National Society of Daughters of the American Revolution
    1776 D Street, N.W.
    Washington, DC 20006-5392
    Tel.: (202) 628-1776

National Society of the Sons of the American Revolution
    5163 Powers Ferry Road
    Atlanta, GA 30327

Palatines to America (Pal-Am)
    Box 101, Capital University
    Columbus, OH 43209

United Daughters of the Confederacy
    Memorial Building
    328 North Boulevard
    Richmond, VA 23220
    Tel.: (804) 355-1636

Sons of Confederate Veterans
    1307 Concord Road
    Smyrna, GA 30080

Periodicals

Canadian Genealogist
    Generation Press
    172 King Henry's Boulevard
    Aigincourt, ON M1T 2V6, Canada

Genealogical Helper
　　P.O. Box 368
　　Logan, UT 84321
　　　　The magazine for every genealogist. General articles ("I Didn't Give Up On My Search For My Family"), a calendar of upcoming genealogical events, Bureau of Missing Ancestors and book reviews are just a few of the regular features in this bi-monthly magazine. Circa 260 pages, index, $4.50 per issue.

Heritage Quest
　　Leland K. Meitzler, editor
　　Drawer 40/114 S. Washington
　　Orting, WA 98360
　　　　Worldwide research, subscriber queries and book reviews. Circa 800 pages published each year, $30.00 per year.

Directories

Directory of Family Associations. Elizabeth Petty Bentley. 1991-92 Edition. Baltimore: Genealogical Publishing Co., Inc., 1991, 318 pages, 8 1/2" by 11", paperback, $29.95.
　　　　More than 10,000 names referring to family associations, publications, reunion committees, one-name societies, surname exchanges and family newsletters. The listings are all in alphabetical order, no categories have been established.
　　　　Address:
　　　　Genealogical Publishing Co., Inc.
　　　　1001 N. Calvert Street
　　　　Baltimore, MD 21202

Directory of Family "One-Name" Periodicals, 1990-91 Edition. Edited by J. Konrad. Munroe Falls: Summit Publications, 1990, 60 pages, 8 1/2" by 11", stapled.
　　　　Lists about 2,000 American and Canadian periodicals dedicated to the research of a single family name, from "All About Abbotts" to the "Zellner Family Quarterly." An "Index of Variant Spellings and Allied Families" cross-references the periodicals.
　　　　Address:
　　　　Summit Publications
　　　　P.O. Box 222
　　　　Munroe Falls, Ohio 44262

Directory of Historical Organizations in the United States and Canada. Edited by Mary Bray Wheeler. 14th edition. Nashville: AASLH Press, 1990, 8 1/2" by 11", 1108 pages, index, paperback.
　　　　Huge directory of associations, libraries, museums, and university departments concerned in any way with historical research and preservation, grouped by state. Includes a name index and a subject index.

Address:
American Association for State and Local History
172 Second Avenue North
Suite 202
Nashville, Tennessee 37201

Directory of Professional Genealogists. Compiled by Eileen Polakoff. Salt Lake City:
Association of Professional Genealogists, 1990, 97 pages, 8 1/2" by 11", paperback,
$15.00.

> Lists nearly 600 members in the United States and eight other countries
> (Australia, Canada, England, Germany, Israel, New Zealand, Sweden, Switzerland). Has helpful information on how to hire a genealogist and a list of
> organizations that have screening programs for professional genealogists.
> Includes cross-reference index to specialties and related services.
> *Address:*
> *Association of Professional Genealogists*
> *P.O. Box 11601*
> *Salt Lake City, Utah 84147-1601*

Genealogical Societies & Historical Societies in the United States, 1990-1991 Edition.
Edited by J. Konrad. Munroe Falls: Summit Publications, 1990, 79 pages, 8 1/2" by
11", stapled.

> Lists more than 3,000 societies in the United States. The same publisher
> also offers a booklet of genealogical and historical societies outside the U.S.
> *Address:*
> *Summit Publications*
> *P.O. Box 222*
> *Munroe Falls, Ohio 44262*

*Meyer's Directory of Genealogical Societies in the U.S.A. and Canada with an appended
list of independent genealogical periodicals endorsed by the Federation of Genealogical Societies and The National Genealogical Society.* Edited by Mary Keysor Meyer.
8th Edition. 1990, 131 pages, 8 1/2" by 11", paperback.

> Lists some 1900 genealogical societies in the United States and Canada,
> including Special Interest (Adoptees, Computer, Afro-American, Belgian etc.),
> Umbrella Groups and Professional Interest Organizations. New section on
> one-name family organizations/newsletters has about 400 entries.
> *Address:*
> *Mary K. Meyer*
> *5179 Perry Road*
> *Mt. Airy, Maryland 21771*
> *Tel.: (301) 875-2824*

Glossary

Abstract

A summary of the most important information in a document, article or book. For instance, an abstract of a deed may relate the names of the people involved, the consideration, a summarized description of the property, warranties, and the nature of the rights transferred, yet not include the legal jargon, the acknowledgement, and the names of the witnesses. (See Extract and Summary)

Administrator (male), Administratrix (female)

A person designated by a court to represent someone who died without an operative will. Usually bonded, an administrator sees to it that the burial is paid for, receivables collected, that debts, taxes, and court costs are paid, and, finally, that the remaining assets of the deceased are properly distributed among his or her heirs. (See Intestate and Bond)

Adoption

A legal process whereby people make someone else's child legally their own. The adoptive parents undertake the duties of natural parents to that child, and the adopted child gains the rights, privileges and duties of a natural child.

Affidavit

A written or printed declaration of facts, made voluntarily and under oath before a person legally empowered to administer oaths, such as a justice of the peace, a notary public, or a lawyer.

Affinity

The relationship between people whose kinship is by marriage, and not "by blood." The relationship between a husband and his wife's relatives is said to be by affinity. (See Consanguinity)

Aforesaid, Beforesaid, Abovesaid, Said

Often used in legal documents, these words refer to a person, object, proposition, or premise previously mentioned in the same document.

Ancestor

Any person from whom one is directly and lineally descended. (See Collateral)

Ancillary

A proceeding which aids, supplements, or complements another proceeding. When, for instance, a decedent owned land not only in the county where he or she lived but in another county as well, the administration in the second county is said to be ancillary to that done in the county of residence. (See Decedent)

Appraisal, Appraisement
An assessment of the value of property, real or personal. In genealogy, the term usually refers to the evaluation of someone's assets at the time of his or her death.

Archives
Usually, the place of keeping for records, writings, mementos, and artifacts having to do with the history of a group of people or a family. Nowadays the term is also used for the records, writings, and mementos themselves.

Asset
Any property, including real property (real estate, interests in land) and personalty (personal property). Personalty is all property other than real estate. In addition to tangible personal property - cattle, refrigerators, tools, etc. - intangible property such as stocks, bonds, negotiable writings, legal claims against others, and accounts receivable are also considered personalty.

Banns, Banns of Matrimony
A requirement in the Church of England and often in the Catholic Church, that a marriage be announced publicly. The announcement is made at service in church, on three consecutive Sundays prior to the proposed date of ceremony. The aim is to allow time for anyone knowing of a good reason against the marriage to come forth.

Beneficiary
Someone who gains profit, advantage, or benefits from another (the benefactor). Someone who inherits from somebody else is said to be that person's beneficiary.

Bond
A sum of money, pledge of credit, insurance guarantee or other thing of value deposited, usually with a court, as assurance that one will faithfully and properly perform certain duties. Administrators of estates are bonded - provide financial assurance - that they will properly attend to and complete the business of the dead person.

Cenotaph
A monument to one who is deceased, positioned elsewhere than at the place of burial. (See Epitaph)

Census
An official counting (enumeration) of all people within a political subdivision (city, county, state, nation). Formerly, a census was taken solely by census-takers (enumerators) who went from door to door listing the names, ages, occupations etc. of the occupants of each dwelling.

Chattel
Any item of property that is not real estate. Chattels are divided into chattels real and chattels personal. Chattels real are tangible goods (guns, dishes, furniture), while

chattels personal are intangible property such as accounts receivable, stocks, bonds, etcetera.

City

In the U.S., a municipality, usually larger than a town or village, which governs itself under a charter granted by a state. Thus, a city is not part of a county yet governs itself in much the same way a county does.

Civil War

That American conflict, also called "The War Between The States" and "The War of the Rebellion," which took place between 1861 and 1865. Other nations (including England, 1642-1646) also have had internal conflicts called civil wars.

Clear and Convincing

A measure of proof beyond "preponderance of evidence." In genealogy, that quantum of evidence that convinces that one hypothesis is almost certainly correct and that no other solution is likely to be found. (See Preponderance of Evidence)

Collateral Branches, Collateral Lines

All relatives who are related to you by blood but not directly (lineally): aunts, uncles, nieces, nephews, etc. The children, grandchildren, etc. of a brother or sister of one of your ancestors, too, are your collateral lines. (See Affinity and Consanguinity)

Colonial

Refers to the period before the American Revolution during which the first thirteen states of the United States were still English colonies. Also refers to the style of architecture, dress, etc. prevalent then in British North America.

Consanguinity

Meaning "of the same blood," the term refers to any person who descends from the same ancestor as you. (See Affinity and Collateral Branches)

Consideration

Refers to anything of value (money, assets, service) that is given in payment for property, real or personal. Love and affection are sufficient consideration - payment - for property if the grantor and grantee so agree.

Constable

A public officer of a town or section of a county whose duties include matters of the peace, the service of writs, and the custody of jurors. While a constable's powers vary from state to state, he usually has considerably less authority than a sheriff. Formerly the constable was a more important officer of the law than now and the title and office were actively sought after.

County

In the U.S., a political subdivision of a state, created to facilitate the administration of justice and law and to permit limited self-government and determination.

County Seat

The town or city within which the county buildings and courts are found, and where the principal business of the county is executed.

Decedent

A dead person; the term usually describes someone who has recently died.

Deed

Any written instrument, signed and delivered, that conveys an interest in real estate from one person to another.

Descendent

Someone who lineally descends from another, no matter through how many generations. Sometimes the term also refers to all those to whom property descends at a death, no matter what the kinship.

Direct Index

An index to the records of deeds and mortgages, usually kept in a courthouse. The Direct Index lists, in alphabetical order by surname, the grantors or mortgagors. Often also called the Grantor Index. (See Reverse Index)

Discharge

As a verb, to discharge a duty or obligation means to fulfill a duty or obligation. As a noun, a discharge is the document that releases a soldier from service and evidences that he or she has performed certain military duties.

Dower

A part of or interest in the estate of a decedent that is reserved by law for the maintenance and support of the deceased's surviving spouse during his or her life. Originally the term dower applied to the real estate gained by the deceased during the marriage.

Dowry

The property a woman brings with her when she marries. Originally, the dowry became the property of the husband at marriage.

Enumeration, Enumerator

Enumeration literally means a counting or numbering and the person who does the numbering is the enumerator. In genealogy, the term enumeration usually refers to a census and the enumerators are the people who "take" the census.

Epitaph

A statement, quotation or verse on a monument or headstone, usually in praise of the deceased.

Estate

All assets, real and personal, belonging to a person, whether living or dead. In genealogy, the term estate usually refers to the assets of a deceased person at the time of his or her death.

Evidence

In genealogy, evidence is considered to be all writings, documents, mementos and artifacts which in any way prove or demonstrate lineage.

Executor (male), Executrix (female)

A person (or persons) who was nominated in a decedent's will (and who was found acceptable by a court) to carry out the terms of that will. The duties of an executor or executrix include arranging the burial of the dead person, collecting all assets owing to him or her, paying all debts and taxes, distributing the remaining assets as prescribed by the will, and then closing the estate.

Extract

A section from a document, letter, book or article, usually taken whole and verbatim from the original. This in contrast to an abstract which repeats only part of the information, or a summary which condenses the information. (See Abstract and Summary)

Foster, Fostered out

A foster parent is someone who carries out the duties of raising a child without legally claiming that child as his or her own. Fostering out is an ancient Irish custom which was carried to the Americas and here modified to an arrangement where a child is given into the custody of another, and, in exchange for care and keeping, is expected to perform the duties expected of a natural child. (See Adoption)

French and Indian War

Conflict between England and its American colonies against France and its allied Indian Nations. The French and Indian War started with a series of incidents in 1754 and ended with the defeat of the French forces at Quebec in 1760, making Canada an English colony.

Genealogy

Genealogy is the study of family history and relationships, both by blood and by marriage. A "genealogy" is a statement, diagram, or summary of kinship.

Genesis

In genealogy, genesis refers to the beginnings and political parentage of any governmental subdivision, specifically those counties or states which were divided up into new counties or states.

Grand

In genealogy, the prefix "grand" refers to the generation prior to your parents. Thus the mother of your mother is your grand-mother, and her sisters and brothers, your great aunts and uncles, are often called "grand aunt" and "grand uncle."

Grantor/Grantee Indexes

Indexes to deeds compiled alphabetically in the surnames of the sellers in the case of a Grantor Index, and in the names of the buyers or transferees in the case of a Grantee Index. (See Direct Index and Reverse Index)

Great

In genealogy, the prefix "great" refers to your ancestors prior to your grandparents. Each generation away from your grandparents has another "great" added. Thus the mother of your grandfather is your great-grandmother, and her father (your grandfather's grandfather) is your great-great-grandfather.

Heir

Presently used to designate any person entitled to inherit from another by right of descent or relationship, whether the death is testate or intestate. Formerly, an heir was someone who inherited by virtue of a statute or law rather than by the provisions of a will.

Hereinafter, Hereinbefore

Legal jargon used to refer to a term or provision within the same document, e.g. "... being the tract hereinafter described" or "... being the persons hereinbefore mentioned."

Holographic Will

A will written, dated, and signed entirely by the decedent in his own hand. Usually, to be legally acceptable a holographic will must have been kept in such a place and maintained with such care that its importance to the decedent is apparent.

Inchoate Rights

Any interest in real estate which has not yet been realized or vested in the owner. In genealogy, the term usually refers to a wife's intangible interests in the real estate of her husband during his life, which may ripen into dower rights at his death. (See Dower)

Indentured Servants

In the American colonies an indenture was a written contract by which a free person would promise to serve someone else as his servant for a term of five to seven years (usually) or until about the age of twenty-five. In exchange for his or her work the indentured servant often received transport across the ocean and certain minimal benefits (clothes, grain, small tracts of land, etc.) at the end of the term.

Indian Wars

The term used to denote the many military conflicts with the American Indians which took place during the last half of the nineteenth century, generally in the western states and territories.

Instant

A term often used in early correspondence, meaning the current month. For instance, a person responding on July 20 to a letter received on July 5 might write: "I acknowledge your letter of the 5th Instant." (See Ultimo)

Intestate

When someone dies without a valid will, he or she is said to have died intestate. The opposite of intestate is testate, which means with a will. (See Administrator, Administratrix)

Inventory

In genealogy, an inventory is usually the list an administrator or executor has made of all property belonging to a decedent at the time of his or her death. (See Appraisal / Appraisement)

Journals, Journal Entries

See Minutes, Minute Books.

Justice of the Peace

A judicial officer having minor authority, usually as to minor crimes, misdemeanors, and matters of the peace. A justice of the peace was an officer of great importance before modern transportation facilitated trips about the county by a sheriff or his deputies.

Kin, Kinship

A loosely defined term referring to any and all of one's relations, be they by affinity, consanguinity, or by law.

Korean Conflict

The conflict between North Korea (and Communist China), and the United States which took place between 1950 and 1953.

Land Grant

In genealogy, a land grant refers to the document or the act whereby a government conveys an interest in land to an individual, corporation or institution. Generally, but not always, the land concerned has not been previously titled to anyone.

Lease

A contract whereby one temporarily grants someone else certain rights, duties and privileges in a tract of land (or in a building, or other property) for a specific period of time. At the end of that term all rights revert back to the original owner.

Letter Patent

See Patent.

Levy

As a verb, to levy a tax means to impose a tax, as in "The colony levied a tax of 1 shilling on each horse used in farming, the same payable to the circuit court in February of each year." As a noun, a levy is the act of imposing or collecting a tax.

Liability

A liability is any obligation, debt, or duty, to pay or to perform to a person, firm, corporation or government.

Lien

When A fails to pay for services rendered or goods supplied by B, B then has a right to place a lien (a claim) against some of A's assets, usually personal property. To be valid under most state's laws, the lien must be written down and recorded.

Lineage
Your lineage is your line of descent from your ancestors, showing the relationship between you, your ancestors and your descendants. The terms "stock" or pedigree are synonymous to lineage.

Litigation
When people take their unresolved disputes to a court for settlement.

Majority
See Of Age.

Manor
Presently, a manor refers to a house that is larger than average. In early times a manor was a grant of a sizable tract of land by the crown, usually to a nobleman.

Marriage Bond
The promise to pay money or something valuable in the event that it is later learned that one of the partners to a marriage was not legally qualified to have married.

Mexican War
Conflict between the United States and Mexico which took place between 1846 and 1848.

Microfiche, Microfilm
A space-saving way to store copies of original documents, books, etc. In the case of microfilm, the older of the two processes, each page is photographed on a roll of film with one page of the original document in each frame. In the case of microfiche, a number of pages are greatly reduced in size and placed on a single sheet of film.

Militia
An armed body of citizens, organized by a state or (early) a colony and, as opposed to an army, active only in cases of civil obedience, local emergency or danger to the public.

Minutes, Minute Books (Orders, Order Books, Journals, Journal Entries)
The minutes are the official records of the sessions of a judicial court, made by the clerks of that court and collected in the minute books.

Mortgage Deed (Mortgagors, Mortgagees)
A formal, signed, and acknowledged document by which a borrower (the mortgagor) conveys the title of his or her property to a lender (the mortgagee) as security for a loan of money or other thing of value. When the mortgagor (the borrower) has paid the debt as agreed, the mortgagee (the lender) then will give the property back, or "release" the title.

A mortgage is similar to a deed of trust, except that in a deed of trust the title is conveyed to a third party agreeable to both lender and borrower, who releases the title back to the mortgagor upon being informed that the debt has been repaid as agreed.

Nativity
In genealogy, nativity means that place where one was born.

Naturalization
The procedure through which the government of one country grants citizenship to a citizen of another country.

Nuncupative Will
An oral will, dictated by one who is dying and, soon after the death, written down and signed by witnesses. Early, on the frontier and in sparsely settled areas, when death often came quickly, nuncupative wills were more frequent than now.

Obituary
An article or (often paid) notice in a newspaper or magazine describing the life, accomplishments, and death of someone who has recently died.

Of Age, Of Majority
The age at which a child becomes an adult, i.e. presumed able and entitled to manage his or her own affairs, and enjoy the full civic privileges and rights afforded by his or her government. These days the achievement of eighteen or twenty-one years is necessary for a child to be considered to have come "of age." In the past, fourteen or even twelve years was considered old enough.

Orders, Order books
See Minutes, Minute Books.

Outcry
Formerly, a sale held by shouting an offer to sell from the courthouse steps to all who might accept the offer and buy. Now, usually a public sale by auction held at a place determined by the owners or a court.

Patent
In genealogy, a document by which a government, state or federal, grants public land; in early records the term Letter Patent frequently appears.

Pedigree
One's lineage or the line of ancestry from which one descends; a chart, account, register, or drawing of one's ancestry.

Per Stirpes
Latin for by roots or by stock. When one inherits that which an ancestor would have inherited had the ancestor been living. For example, when a granddaughter inherits from her grandmother what her father would have inherited had he outlived his mother.

Personalty, Personal Property
All property other than real estate. (See Assets)

Political Subdivision

A term used to describe a division of a larger political boundary, e.g., a county usually is a political subdivision of a state, and a township usually is a political subdivision of a county.

Poll

People singly considered ('poll' originally meant 'head'), as in a "poll tax" where a tax is levied on each individual (on each head).

Polls

The place where people cast ballots; a voting place.

Precinct

In America, usually a rather small area in a town or city designated as an election or voting district.

Preponderance of Evidence

A measure of proof. When the evidence tending to prove one hypothesis outweighs, even minimally, the evidence tending to prove a contrary hypothesis, the first hypothesis is said to win by a preponderance of evidence.

In genealogy, preponderance of evidence is the measure of proof thought sufficient by some to establish lineage, but not by all. (See Clear and Convincing)

Primogeniture

The superior and exclusive right of the first born male to succeed to the family property. A doctrine manifest in many early colonial estates by which the eldest son, or his eldest son, etc., inherited the family property to the exclusion of all sisters, brothers, widows, etc., without regard to need.

Probate, Probate Courts

Probate usually means the legal process by which a will is proved and enforced but can refer to any legal process involving estates. Probate Courts generally have jurisdiction in matters of death, orphans, adoption, children, lunacy, etc.

Quit-claim

Often inaccurately called a quit-claim deed; an instrument by which one transfers whatever interest one may have in some property, usually real estate, to someone else.

Reader

In genealogy, the optical equipment used to read microfilm or microfiche.

Real Estate, Real Property, Realty

Refers to interests in or ownership of land, as opposed to personal property.

Record (to record)

The act of entering any document or writing into the public record by a clerk, recorder, register of deeds, etc., in accordance with a "recording statute." Recording is an innovation peculiar to the American colonies and was not previously found in England.

Redemptioner

Someone who promised his or her labor to a speculator in payment - redemption - for transportation to the colonies and sometimes a tract of land. (See Indentured Servant)

Revolutionary War

The conflict between the American Colonies and England which took place between 1775 and 1783 and which resulted in the formation of the United States.

Scribe, Scrivener

A writer. Before literacy was widespread a scribe was someone whose occupation was writing for others. The surname Scribner derives from the term.

Section

See Township.

Sheriff

Usually, the chief administrative and peace officer of a county. His duties consist of assisting all courts of general jurisdiction, summoning juries, serving writs and executing court orders. The office of sheriff is an ancient office, recorded in England before the 12th century. There the "High Sheriff" had wide authority and jurisdiction within a county, and spoke for the crown, the courts, and government in general.

Sibling

From the early Saxon "sibb" which meant a relative or kinsman. Now the term is used only to refer to brothers and sisters.

Spanish-American War

Conflict between the United States and Spain which took place in 1898.

Spouse

One's wife or husband.

Stock

In genealogy, one's ancestry or lineage, from which arises the expression, "That family is from good stock."

Summary

A writing that, with different wording, sets forth the significant portions of another document, article, book, or source. (See Abstract and Extract)

Surety

Someone who gives assurance that another person will pay or appear as agreed or ordered. Usually a surety posts personal credit, a "surety bond", consisting of money or something of value as a guarantee.

Testate

Death with an operative will, as opposed to intestate which means death without a will. (See Executor, Executrix)

Tithe, Tithable

Early, a tax-like charge of ten percent to the benefit of the church. In America, the tithe was based on benefits and income derived from land and its use. One is tithable when one is required to pay tithes.

Title

The word title has two meanings. In the context of real estate and personal property, to "hold title" to something means that one owns that something.

Socially, a title designates a measure of respect or dignity due to a person, e.g., Mr., Mrs., Lord, Judge, etc.

Town

Usually a civil and political subdivision of a county. In New England, a town usually has the powers and authority only accorded to counties in other states. In some states, a town is a village or hamlet within a township.

Township

In lands previously belonging to the U.S. government, a township is a division of land 6 miles long on each side, containing 36 sections of 640 acres (1 square mile) each. In some states, a township refers to a political subdivision of a county and it may or may not consist of 36 square miles.

Transcript

A verbatim record or exact copy of a document, book, or other writing; e.g. "A transcript of the county's Marriage Records was made available to researchers."

Trust deed

See Mortgage Deed.

Ultimo (Ult.)

A term often used in early correspondence, Ultimo is short for the Latin "ultimo mense" which means "in the last month." For instance, a person responding in March to a letter received on February 17 might write: "I received your note of the 17th Ult." (See Instant)

Vendee, Vendor

A vendee is a buyer and a vendor a seller of personal property (personalty).

Veteran

In genealogy, anyone who served in any military or militia unit (under federal, state or territorial government) for any period of time, and who was honorably separated from that service unit. It makes no difference whether the service was by conscription (draft) or voluntarily.

Vital Statistics

Usually refers to the data maintained by government - state or federal - on births, deaths, and marriages. "Bureaus of Vital Statistics" have been operating in every state since the early years of the twentieth century and are open to the public.

War of 1812

The conflict between the United States and Great Britain which took place between 1812 and 1814.

Ward

A political subdivision of a city or town, having limited jurisdiction in matters of voting and election, sanitary regulations, fire and police protection, and enumerations.

Warranty Deed

A written document transferring interests in land and containing specific warranties concerning the extent of the rights transferred. The most common deeds in this country, warranty deeds contain a complete description of the property, set forth the names of the buyers and the sellers, are acknowledged ("notarized", "sworn to"), almost always recorded, and often, especially early, contain a recital of the consideration given in exchange for the property.

Will

A formal writing, carefully governed by all states, by which one directs and sets forth one's wishes concerning the disposition of one's estate at death. A will usually names and empowers an executor or executrix; gives directions concerning burial, collection of receivables and payment of bills and taxes; names all beneficiaries and disposes of the remainder of the estate. To be legal, a will usually must be signed, acknowledged, and witnessed. (See Executor, Executrix; Nuncupative Wills; and Holographic Wills)

World War I

World-wide conflict of 1914 - 1918 in which the United States took part from 1917 until 1918.

World War II

World-wide conflict of 1939 - 1945 in which the United States took part from December of 1941 until August of 1945.

Writ

In genealogy, any order by a court in the name of a government - federal, state or local - addressed to a sheriff or other law officer. Often, a writ will direct an officer to notify someone of an action filed against him or her and instruct them to appear at a certain time and place to answer to the charge or complaint. Writs are common genealogical source documents.

Index

About the Author

Paul Drake, J.D., has degrees in history and law and has been doing genealogical and historical research for forty-five years. An accomplished and recognized lecturer and teacher at Roane State College and, formerly, at Tennessee Technical University, Dr. Drake has written two books and numerous articles concerning the Civil War, historical research and evidence, and genealogy (for both the beginning and the advanced researcher), which have been published in various state and national journals.

Dr. Drake, a grandfather several times over, is semi-retired and lives with his wife, Marty, their two dogs, and his collection of historical newspapers and mementos in the mountains at Crab Orchard, Tennessee.